World War II Wargames Rules

BOLT ACTION

MW00527635

DUEL IN THE SUN

The African and Italian Campaigns

Written by: Dylan Owen and
Alessio Cavatore

Edited by: Paul Sawyer and
Rick Priestley

Cover artwork: Peter Dennis

Interior artwork: Steve Noon, Peter Dennis,
Howard Gerrard, Stephen Andrew,
Johnny Shumate and Michael Welply

Photography: Michael Perry, Mark Owen,
Warwick Kinrade and Gabrio Tolentino

Miniatures painted by: Gary Martin, Bruce Murray, Andres Amian,
Alan Mander, Neil Burt, Jose Bustamante, Darek Wyrozebski, Mark Owen,
Darren Linington, Rafa Archiduque, Mark Hargreves (Over Open Sights),
Colin Dixon and Michael Perry

Miniatures supplied by: Warlord Games,
Perry Minatures and Blitzkrieg Minatures

Thanks to: John Stallard

OSPREY
PUBLISHING

WARLORD
GAMES

ospreypublishing.com
warlordgames.com

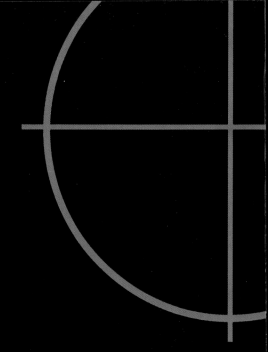

First published in Great Britain in 2016 by Osprey Publishing
Kemp House, Chawley Park, Cumnor Hill, Oxford OX2 9PH, UK
29 Earlsfort Terrace, Dublin 2, Ireland
PO Box 3985, New York, NY 10185–3985, USA
Email: info@ospreypublishing.com

Osprey Publishing, part of Bloomsbury Publishing Plc

Warlord Games
T13/T15 Technology Wing, The Howitt Building, Lenton Business Centre, Lenton Boulevard,
Nottingham, NG7 2BD, UK
Email: info@warlordgames.com

A CIP catalogue record for this book is available from the British Library

Print ISBN: 978 1 4728 0742 7
PDF e-book ISBN: 978 1 4728 1370 1
EPUB e-book ISBN: 978 1 4728 1371 8

Page layout by PDQ Media, Bungay, UK
Typeset in Univers and Nidex
Originated by PDQ Media, Bungay, UK
Printed and bound in India by Replika Press Private Ltd.

23 24   10 9 8 7 6 5

Osprey Publishing supports the Woodland Trust, the UK's leading woodland conservation charity.
Between 2014 and 2018 our donations were spent on their Centenary Woods project in the UK.
www.ospreypublishing.com

For more information on **Bolt Action** and other products, please visit **www.warlordgames.com**

CONTENTS

WHAT IS THIS BOOK?

The 4th Indian Division applies pressure to the Mareth Line defences with an outflanking attack through the Matmata Hills, by

BLOOD IN THE MEDITERRANEAN

The beginning of 1940 was a dark time for the Great Britain. The Phoney War against Germany had given way to the humiliating retreat from Dunkirk, where Britain abandoned mainland Europe to Hitler's seemingly unstoppable armies. The threat of a Nazi invasion of Great Britain receded following the heroic sacrifices of the Allied pilots who won the Battle of Britain in the summer of 1940, but the first bombs of the Blitz had begun to shatter London and no part of the entire country felt secure from the threat of the Luftwaffe.

Britain's new Prime Minister, Winston Churchill, badly needed a demonstration of strength against Germany to lift morale and to show the world that British forces could fight back against the Nazi menace. Western Europe was too well-defended – as proved by costly forays against Nazi-occupied France and Norway. But the northern coasts of Africa, recently claimed as colonial territories by fascist Italy, were a potential target for a counter-attack by the forces of the British

Empire stationed in Egypt, who were already engaged with Italian troops. A swift series of victories against Germany's closest ally would raise spirits back home in Blighty, as well as weaken the grip of fascism on the Mediterranean.

And so Churchill moved his chess piece across the Mediterranean board, setting in motion a chain of events that would lead to tragedy in Greece, triumph in the face of near-defeat in the sands of Egypt and eventually the overthrow of Mussolini.

This supplement for the tabletop wargame *Bolt Action* covers the land battles that raged across the Mediterranean from 1940 to 1944. Though certainly not a definitive history of this period of World War II, it gives an overview of the major battles fought in this region, and highlights specific events that make exciting and challenging games for those who want to play out this part of the global conflict with their *Bolt Action* armies.

Over open sights! 25-pdrs take on the German offensive.

Within these pages, you'll find five sections dedicated to the different phases of the war in the Mediterranean:

- The initial clashes between the British and Italian armies in Libya, and Britain's first unexpected victories.
- The ill-fated British expedition to protect Greece from Hitler's invading troops, and the subsequent desperate battles of British and Commonwealth forces in Crete against determined German paratroopers.
- The epic tank duels in the deserts of North Africa as Hitler reinforced Mussolini's battered forces with the deadly Afrika Korps, and the ultimate showdown between two legendary desert commanders, Rommel and Montgomery, at El Alamein.
- The debut of the Americans into the African theatre, their bloody setback at Kasserine Pass, and eventual success in helping to clear North Africa of Axis influence.
- The Allied invasions of Sicily and mainland Italy, and the stubborn German defence that resisted the invaders almost up to the end of the war in Europe.

Each section includes a brief overview of important events, *Bolt Action* scenarios based on significant battles or typical actions, as well as details on the forces

available to fight them. Also, special rules appropriate to that particular theatre of war, such as amphibious assaults, paratroop drops or environmental effects, plus details on special units that fought in those battles, for example, the Hermann Göring Division, the Gurkhas and the forces of the Free French. Interspersed among these sections are rules for fielding some of the renowned individuals whose exploits in these battles won them fame (or infamy).

In many ways, the battles fought in the burning sands of North Africa, the mountains of Greece and the freezing mud of the Winter Line in Italy were overshadowed by the massive, meat-grinding conflict on the Eastern Front, the Allied advance through Western Europe following the Normandy landings, and the suffocating horror of jungle warfare in the Pacific. But for the wargamer, the Mediterranean theatre is a fantastic conflict to re-enact on the tabletop. It deployed a range of often exotic forces (ten nationalities were involved in the final Allied push against the German troops defending the Winter Line). And if you want battles pitting unusual forces against each other, look no further than these pages (US Army versus Vichy French, anyone?). And depending on the size of your model collection and range of your tabletop terrain, you can refight the many tank battles that swept through the Libyan Desert, or battle it out in a thrilling mountaintop skirmish in the depths of the Apennine winter.

So onwards to war! And let it never be said, as Churchill optimistically claimed, that your Mediterranean adventures take place in the soft underbelly of the Axis. Your battles here will be a fierce challenge.

Rommel's command half-track, 'Greif'

MUSSOLINI STRIKES

Infantry, with armoured support, charge across the North African terrain, by Steve Noon © Osprey Publishing Ltd. Taken from Warrior 160: Desert Rat 1940–43.

Hitler never intended his war to spill into the Mediterranean. His initial aim was total German control over Europe – North Africa was an irrelevant backwater as far the German high command was concerned. But on 6 February 1941, Hitler appointed *Generalleutnant* Erwin Rommel as commander of the newly created *Deutsches Afrika Korps*, and a week later the first wave of German troops set foot in Tripoli, colonial capital of Italian Libya. The Axis boot-print would not be erased from the North African sands before two long years of fighting.

It was the grandiose schemes of the Italian fascist dictator, Benito Mussolini, that drew Germany into the North African conflict. Yet Mussolini's decision to open a new front of the war in the Mediterranean's North African littoral zone was the result of his determination to prove to the world that Italy was as much a resurgent European power as Germany – an aggressive successor to the ailing democracies of old Europe, the 'Roman Empire' reborn. Mussolini planned to wage a 'parallel war' alongside, not subordinate to, his fellow fascist allies, and hoped to share in the spoils of war as equal victors.

The two Axis powers had signed the Pact of Steel in May 1939, obligating both countries to help each other militarily. However, Germany's invasion of Poland later that year took Mussolini by surprise – he had not expected Hitler to unleash his forces until at least 1941, and the Germans had not informed him of their intentions. He stayed out of the war. In truth, despite Mussolini's belligerent rhetoric, Italy was unready for war. The majority of her fighting forces were poorly trained, poorly motivated, poorly equipped and often poorly led. In comparison with the powerhouses of Germany and the British Empire, she was economically and militarily inferior.

THE PARALLEL WAR

It was not until the rapid collapse of the French and the humiliation of the British in Belgium and France in the face of the German Blitzkrieg, that Mussolini decided to fight. On 10 June 1940, he declared war on Britain and France, convinced that Germany had already struck the deathblow and eager to claw some glory and war booty from the stricken nations before they surrendered. In his words: "Italy only needs a few thousand dead in order to sit at the negotiating table".

However, the initial Italian attack into French territory failed to break through the mountain forts of the Alpine Line and made only a little better progress along the coast. By the time France surrendered to Germany on 24 June, Italy had made little headway, capturing only a thin line of French territory along the border between the two countries. Bad weather, bad terrain and bad planning had stalled Mussolini's first foray into the war. Of the 6,000 casualties suffered by Italy that June, a third were hospitalised due to frostbite from the freezing Alpine conditions – a sure indication of the unpreparedness of her armies and incompetence of Mussolini's military commanders.

Mussolini had to look elsewhere to win his laurels. Africa was his obvious choice: Italy had a North African colony in Libya, as well as Eritrea and Somalia in East Africa. Abyssinia (modern Ethiopia), had recently been conquered by Mussolini in 1936, and he was eager to expand his African influence at the expense of Britain and France.

Italians advance across the dusty wilderness.

Marshal Balbo, governor-general of Libya and commander of Italy's African armies, was more aware of his force's shortcomings than their leader was, so he procrastinated – he wanted to invade British-controlled Egypt only after Germany's expected invasion of England. However, the initiative was seized from him when a mere three days after Mussolini's declaration of hostilities, the 11th Hussars swept from Egypt into Libya in a lightning raid. In Rolls-Royce armoured cars, they swiftly seized the Italian border forts Maddalena and Capuzzo, and then proceeded to capture an Italian general on the road to Tobruk, who was carrying detailed plans of the defences of the important sea port of Bardia.

Before Balbo could respond, he became an early casualty of the North African conflict, his plane shot down by over-zealous Italian anti-aircraft gunners at Tobruk, a strategically-sited Libyan port near the Egyptian border. He was replaced by Marshal Rodolfo Graziani, the ruthless pacifier of Libya and conqueror of Abyssinia. On 15 July, Mussolini commanded his new marshal to organise an attack against the Egyptian port of Alexandria, but Graziani kept on postponing the invasion, although numerous skirmishes took place across the Libyan-Egyptian border between the Italians and the British 8th Army based in Egypt. Only when Graziani was threatened with demotion did he advance five divisions of the 10th Army into Egyptian territory on 13 September. The British were greatly outnumbered, as potential reinforcements remained in the UK to defend against the imminent German invasion, and the defenders engaged in an orderly fighting retreat, harassing the Italians from the air and with light forces of motorised infantry, light artillery batteries and armoured cars. The Italians recaptured Fort

Capuzzo, but could only advance as far as the town of Sidi Barrani, a mere 60 miles from the Libyan frontier, due to a lack of supplies. This was to be an ongoing problem for both sides of the North African conflict throughout the campaign, as victorious armies stretched their lines of communication too thin across hundreds of miles of sparsely populated desert.

The Italian's modest success in Egypt followed a victory by Mussolini's East African army. During August, while Graziani dithered in Libya, the Duke of Aosta, viceroy of Italian East Africa, overwhelmed British Somalia with a massive force of mainly native troops. However, with Italian shipping barred from the Suez Canal, the Duke's army was isolated, and his conquest of a minor Imperial colony gained little overall advantage.

While Mussolini's African armies consolidated their positions, the dictator's eyes turned towards Greece and the Balkans. Hitler had been sending troops to aid the fascist dictatorship rising in Romania. Uninformed of this until after the occasion, Mussolini's ire at Hitler treating him as a junior partner in the conquest of Europe influenced his rash decision to attack Greece in October, to prove to Hitler that Italy could win conquests of its own in Europe. By mid-November, the invasion of Greece, launched from Italian-controlled Albania, had broken against the wintry steadfasts of the Epirus mountains, and Mussolini's beleaguered forces were swept back deep into Albania by the Greek counter-attack. The botched invasion had diverted much-needed men and materiel from the North African advance. The push into Egypt was postponed and troops sent to reinforce Albania. The Italian army had now stalled on all fronts.

FORGING A NEW ROMAN EMPIRE USING *BOLT ACTION*.

If you want to see if you can do a better job than Mussolini did at grabbing land from the French, subjugating Greece and overthrowing British rule in Egypt and East Africa, use the following guidelines to set up your forces and play the battles.

SCENARIOS

GENERAL SCENARIOS
The following scenarios from the *Bolt Action* rulebook are particularly suited to the kind of actions that the Italian army fought during this preliminary stage of Mussolini's war:

- Scenario 1: Envelopment (page 108) – France, Greece, East Africa
- Scenario 2: Maximum Attrition (page 110) – Greece, North Africa, East Africa
- Scenario 3: Point Defence (page 112) – France, Greece, North Africa, East Africa
- Scenario 4: Hold Until Relieved (page 114) – France, Greece, East Africa

The Italians are the attackers in all these scenarios, where applicable. Of course, if you want to represent one of the localized counter-attacks by Allied forces, the Italians can also be used as the defenders.

In the Alps and Greece, the following scenario from this supplement is also applicable due to the mountainous nature of the terrain:

• Control the Heights (page 82)

In North Africa, use the scenarios on pages 17–20 to represent the Italians' initial successful attack against the British – of course the tables have not yet been turned on them, so the Italians are the attackers and the British are the defenders.

TERRAIN
Although geographically distant, the battlegrounds in the Alps and the Pindus mountain ranges consisted of similar rugged, highland terrain. To represent the fact that many battles were fought along river valleys or through mountain passes, you might want to play scenarios lengthways along the tabletop, with players facing each across the short table edges. The long table edges are flanked by impassable mountains, so outflanking manoeuvres are not allowed.

Try to fill the tabletop with lots of rocky hills, escarpments, gullies, boulders and impassable rivers, for example, that will slow down infantry and impede the movement of other types of unit. These regions are sparsely inhabited, so few civilian buildings should be on the board. For the Pindus region, you might also want to include marshy terrain where a battle is being fought alongside a river or in a low-lying area.

The Greek and French borders were defended by many fortified bunkers, pillboxes and concrete emplacements, so in scenarios where the Greek or French player has a 'Defender's Set-up Zone', he can place one bunker anywhere in this zone.

In Greece, the few roads through the mountains were poorly maintained, so a vehicle moving along a road can only double its move rate on the D6 score of a 4+, tested every time it moves.

Autumn rains and low cloud rendered the Italian superiority in air power almost useless – during a game in the Greek theatre, one player rolls a die before the set-up phase. On a 1–5, for the duration of the game, neither player can call down an airstrike due to bad weather. To represent the incessant rain churning up the ground, you could use the rules for fighting in mud on page 136.

The French campaign was fought amidst the snow of the Alpine springtime. If you want to represent this, the entire tabletop counts as rough ground, except to units equipped with skis. The Italians were woefully underequipped to fight in this mountainous region, and to represent casualties from frostbite, all Italians fighting in the French Alps use the Frostbite rules (see page 136). Note that French units are not affected by frostbite – it's assumed they are adequately prepared for the hostile environment.

For battles fought in the deserts of Egypt, see page 121 for details on how to set up desert battles, and desert environmental effects.

The terrain in East Africa consists of mainly steppe lands – grass, brush and thicket, perhaps dotted with a few native huts and some low hills.

ITALIAN FORCES
If you're fielding the Italians, use the following theatre selectors:

1940–41: INVASION OF GREECE
Page 30 of the *Armies of Italy and the Axis* supplement. Obviously, this is the theatre selector to use for any action fought during the Greek campaign. This selector can also be used to represent the forces fighting the brief war against the French in the Alps (additional suitable theatre selectors for this are available in the *Germany Strikes* supplement for *Bolt Action*).

1940–43: THE WAR IN AFRICA
Page 31 of the *Armies of Italy and the Axis* supplement. This selector is used to represent armies attacking the British in Egypt in 1940, with the following restrictions:

• You cannot choose *Paracadutisti* infantry sections (not formed until September 1941).
• In Greece and North Africa, you can add a captured Renault R35 to your choice of tanks.
• It's too early in the war to be able to choose any self-propelled guns.
• You cannot field an Autoblinda 41 or a Sahariana, or an Autoprotetto S37.

A War in Africa Reinforced Platoon can also be used to represent the Duke of Aosta's East African Army. This follows the same restrictions as described above, with the additional restriction that you can only field 0–1 of ANY infantry section apart from Colonial troops – this is to reflect the fact that 70% of the East African Army comprised of askaris (professional colonial soldiers) from Eritrea, Somalia and Abyssinia (Ethiopia), led by Italian officers.

Eritrean regulars and the Somalians of the Royal Corps of Colonial Troops were among the best Italian units in the region, and you can field these by upgrading any Colonial Troop units to Regular for +3pts per man. The Royal Corps included courageous Eritrean cavalry known as Falcon Feathers.

Somali Dubats were skilled skirmishers. You can upgrade one Colonial Troop unit to Dubats expert skirmishers at a cost of +2pts per man. When outflanking as described on page 119 of the *Bolt Action* rulebook, Dubats units may enter from either the left/right table edge as normal, or even from the enemy's own table edge!

Italian forces, Libya 1940–41 (L–R): Soldato, 64th Artillery Regt, 'Catanzaro' Inf Div; Muntaz, 3rd Bn 'Nalut', 4th Group, 2nd Libyan Div; Primo capo squadra, 231st Legion, '28 Ottobre' MVSN Div, by Stephen Andrew © Osprey Publishing Ltd. Taken from Men-at-Arms 349: The Italian Army 1940–45 (2).

Italian Army squad

Some Abyssinian conscripts were prone to desertion. Abyssinian colonial infantry sections may be given the Shirkers special rule at a cost of –3pts per man.

The Duke of Aosta's army was reinforced by the German Motorized Company, a small force of Germans who had fled British-held Kenya and Tanganyika at the start of the war. Transported by trucks, the company was accompanied be a few improvised armoured cars. This force can be represented by one truck-mounted Inexperienced German infantry squad (*Bolt Action*, pages 129–30) and one Inexperienced SDKFZ 222 light armoured car (*Bolt Action*, page 141). The German infantry are not affected by (but are counted for) the Italian 'Avanti Savoia!' rule (*Armies of Italy and the Axis*, page 11).

ALLIED FORCES

The French facing the opportunistic Italian invasion can be represented by a Defence of Vichy Reinforced Platoon (see page 36 of the *Armies of France and the Allies* supplement).

The Greeks defending their homeland against Italian attack can be represented by a Battle of Greece Reinforced Platoon (see page 94 of the *Armies of France and the Allies* supplement).

The British Western Desert Force in Egypt can be represented by an *Operation* Compass Reinforced Platoon (see page 72 of the *Armies of Great Britain* supplement).

The British force fighting the Duke of Aosta's army can be represented by an East Africa Reinforced Platoon (see page 71 of the *Armies of Great Britain* supplement).

CAMELRY

A few (*very* few) units used camels as cavalry mounts, such as the Somaliland Camel Corps fighting on the British side in the East African theatre (mechanised in 1942), the *méharistes* of Le Clerc's Free French and the Indian Bikaner Camel Corps, which fought in the Middle East (beyond the scope of this supplement).

You can field the Somaliland Camel Corps in an East Africa Reinforced Platoon (see the *Armies of Great Britain* supplement, page 71) by giving one or more Regular infantry sections in the platoon the Cavalry special rule for +2pts per man. The unit ignores the penalties for moving through natural rough ground in battles fought in the East African steppe lands.

You can field the French *méharistes* in a Defence of Vichy Reinforced Platoon (see page 36 of the *Armies of France and the Allies* supplement) by giving one or more Moroccan Goumier sections in the platoon the Cavalry special rule for +2 pts per man. The unit ignores the penalties for moving through natural rough ground in battles fought in the North African deserts. Be warned, however, that putting such an exotic unit on the table might raise a few eyebrows…

OPERATION *COMPASS*

The British retreat into Egypt in the face of overwhelming odds was a deliberate and well-executed plan, designed to slow down and harass the superior forces of the invaders. That the pursuit halted so abruptly at Sidi Barrani revealed to the British commander-in-chief of the Middle East, General Sir Archibald Wavell, the supply and logistics predicament faced by the army he opposed. But Wavell had his own problems; his 30,000 men in Egypt faced over 150,000 Italians in Libya. However, Wavell was undeterred – the Western Desert Force that he controlled was much better equipped and trained, and better motivated.

The field commander of the British force, Lieutenant General Richard O'Connor, was not a man to let a minor matter such as apparently insurmountable odds daunt him. On 9 December, Wavell unleashed O'Connor and his troops to enact Operation *Compass*, a fast-moving assault intended to push the Italians from western Egypt and back through Libya.

Speed and surprise were vital to success, as well as the careful planning of resources. Supply dumps had been concealed in the desert along the proposed lines of advance, and the mission was kept highly secret.

The attack was initiated by a spearhead of Matilda tanks from the 7th Royal Tank Regiment attacking the Italian fortified camps that ringed Sidi Barrani, closely followed by the 4th Indian Division. The Royal Navy provided close gunnery support from the coast. The attack achieved complete surprise and the Italian positions were easily taken. Sidi Barrani was seized the next day, and four Italian divisions surrendered on 11 December.

A detachment of the 7th Armoured Division (more famously known as the 'Desert Rats') then cut the coast road between Sidi Barrani and Buqbuq, while the main force of the division attacked the Catanzaro Division in front of Buqbuq, destroying the Italian force and capturing the town. Meanwhile, the Italian Cirene Division, 40km south of Sidi Barrani, retreated to defend the Halfaya Pass.

At a cost of 600 casualties, the British had captured almost 40,000 enemy troops, and over 200 field guns and 70 tanks.

BARDIA AND TOBRUK

O'Connor's sights were set next on the port of Bardia, on the border between Egypt and Libya, and a vital nexus of communication. He was ready to launch his next major attack on 3 January 1941. The 7th Armoured Division was at the forefront of the attack once more, but replacing the Indian 4th Division (moved to the Sudan to face the Duke of Aosta's Abyssinian forces) was the newly arrived Australian 6th Division. It was another bold move by O'Connor. Marshal Graziani had six divisions defending Bardia, but after a three-day battle, the Italians surrendered, confounded by O'Connor's skill at attacking from the least expected direction with his highly mobile force, and his ability to ensure that his infantry and tanks fought as one. Here, the British and Commonwealth forces lost fewer than 500 casualties, while capturing another 40,000 prisoners, over 450 guns, and 127 tanks.

The 7th Armoured Division sped onwards in an attempt to cut off the port of Tobruk, supported by two Australian brigades. Despite being heavily fortified, Tobruk surrendered on 22 January, giving up 25,000 men, 200 guns and nearly 90 tanks.

The division proceeded towards the Gulf of Sirte, south of Benghazi, to enclose and then destroy the bulk of the Italian armies in Cyrenaica, a peninsula surrounded on three sides by the Mediterranean.

However, by this time, the British were suffering acute shortages due to overstretched supply lines and increasingly fragile lines of communication. Their spectacular advance had taken them 1,300km from Cairo, and many of their tanks were now unserviceable. Would they be able to finish off the Italians before their attack ground to a halt?

EAST AFRICA: THE EMPIRE FIGHTS BACK

While the Desert Rats were rolling up the Italian lines in the sands of North Africa, the colonial possessions of the Italians in East Africa were being harried from neighbouring British colonies.

Mussolini's boys charge out of the blue.

On 19 January, the 4th Indian Division, fresh from the North African desert, led by Major General William Platt, attacked the Duke of Aorta's army in Abyssinia. Major General Alan Cunningham ordered a simultaneous attack from Kenya against the Duke's southern lines. Aosta's army was isolated and crippled by a lack of supplies, due to the British closing the Suez Canal to Italian shipping.

You can fight out actions from this campaign on the tabletop using the East Africa Reinforced Platoon from *Armies of Great Britain*, and The War in Africa Reinforced Platoon from *Armies of Italy and the Axis*, modified as described on page 11. The 4th Indian Division (or 5th Indian Division which was also involved) can be represented by an Indian Division Reinforced Platoon (page 23).

THE BENGHAZI HANDICAP

The remnants of the Italian 10th Army, led by General Berganzoli, began to evacuate Cyrenaica, harried by the Royal Air Force, which had achieved air superiority after a succession of victories over Italian planes. On 4 February, while the 6th Australian Division pursued the retreating enemy along the coast road, the 7th Armoured Division raced through the desert to cut off the Italian withdrawal.

On 5 February, at Beda Fomm, a column of tanks from the 11th Hussars, along with the 2nd Battalion of the Rifle Brigade and three batteries of Royal Horse Artillery, intercepted the vanguard of Berganzoli's 20,000-strong force. Desperate to

break through the British lines to safety, the Italians attempted attack after attack against the front of the Rifle Brigade, but were each time repulsed. Hundreds perished before the rapid fire of the stubborn British rifles. Hundreds threw down their arms and surrendered. After three hours of fierce fighting, the tanks of the 7th Hussars thundered in against the left and rear of the leading Italian columns. Panic set in among the Italians, and only nightfall saved them from destruction.

On 6 February, at dawn, reinforcing Italian tanks arrived, and Berganzoli tried another breakout with infantry and armour. More squadrons of the 7th Armoured Division bolstered the British lines, and at the end of a fierce firefight that lasted all day, over a hundred Italian tanks had been knocked out. That night, the Italians attempted nine times to smash aside the British, but to no avail. When a final push at dawn failed, faced with the prospect of the 6th Australian Division attacking from behind after seizing Benghazi the day before, General Berganzoli surrendered his entire army to a victorious force a quarter its size.

ENTER ROMMEL

On 12 February, a new player entered the North African arena. At Hitler's behest, following pleas from a frantic Mussolini, *Generalleutnant* Erwin Rommel landed in Tripoli with advance elements of his Afrika Korps. The North African campaign had entered a new and, for the British, deadlier phase.

FIGHTING OPERATION *COMPASS* USING *BOLT ACTION*

General Wavell's initial plan was for a "Short and swift" operation that lasted for "four or five days at the most, and taking every advantage of the element of surprise."

O'Connor certainly used the element of surprise to full advantage. His aims were to force the Italians to retreat from the defensive camps they had set up after reaching Sidi Barrani, so as to retake the lost ground and, importantly, re-secure the airfields in the area – vital for British air superiority throughout the Mediterranean. As it was, O'Connor greatly exceeded his initial orders, taking advantage of his astounding successes and turned the raid into a full-blown invasion of Italian Libya, conquering as far as Benghazi, 600km from the Egyptian border.

The first part of the operation included an attack

on Italian positions in Egypt, first at Nibeiwa then Tummar and Sidi Barrani. The defeated Italians abandoned their camps at Sofafi-Rabia and Khur-Samalus, and the British pressed on their advantage by capturing Bardia, just across the Libyan border, then Tobruk and finally Benghazi.

The 7th Armoured Division fought throughout the operation, fielding Matilda tanks. The 4th Indian Division (to which were attached the 2nd Cameron Highlanders) fought in the campaign until after the capture of Sidi Barrani, at which point they were hurried to reinforce British troops in East Africa, and the 6th Australian Division took over.

Using the *Bolt Action* rules, you can refight actions from *Operation* Compass by following the suggestions detailed below.

THEATRE SELECTORS

The following forces should be used to represent the armies involved in Operation *Compass*:

ITALIANS

• War in Africa Reinforced Platoon (*Armies of Italy and the Axis*, page 31).

BRITISH & COMMONWEALTH

• Operation *Compass* Reinforced Platoon (*Armies of Great Britain*, page 72).
• Behind Enemy Lines Reinforced Platoon (*Armies of Great Britain*, page 73) – represents units sent to disrupt enemy defences deep inside Italian territory.
• Indian Division Reinforced Platoon (page 23).

OPERATION *COMPASS* SPECIAL RULES

The following special rules are pertinent to battles fought in this campaign (though the Battle of Beda Fomm, on page 17, has its own set of special rules):

DESERT WARFARE

Operation *Compass* was fought in the Egyptian/Libyan desert. See the rules for Desert Warfare, on page 121.

DESERT FIGHTERS

The 7th Armoured Division, having been formed to protect Egypt back in 1938, were already trained in desert warfare – all tanks in British reinforced platoons have the Desert Fighters rule (see page 122). No other British units are yet experienced enough in desert warfare to have the rule.

None of the Italians count as having the Desert Fighters rule. Although some units would have had several years of experience in desert conditions, this is offset by the generally poor state of their equipment.

THE ELEMENT OF SURPRISE

Major-General O'Connor, commander of Operation *Compass*, was a master at conducting surprise attacks against the Italians. He always attacked at first light, and always seemed to carry off the element of surprise.

In any game set during Operation *Compass*, the British player can decide to attack at dawn, using the Dawn Assault rules (see page 129).

When implementing the Blindside rule (page 122) during a Dawn Assault, the British player uses O'Connor's Officer Morale modifier (+6) rather than that of the commanding officer of his platoon.

In addition, the British side ignores the Dust Trail rule (page 122), due to the Italians' lack of proper reconnaissance and O'Connor's seemingly inexhaustible luck.

Also, in the first turn of the game, every time an Italian order die is drawn, it is replaced and another die is drawn – if that second die is an Italian one, it is not replaced.

"EIGHT MILLION BAYONETS"

Graziani's infantry vastly outnumbered the British. To represent this (and to make things a bit more balanced for the Italians after all the disadvantages they are suffering) for every Regular or Inexperienced Infantry Section bought for the Italian platoon, the Italian player can field an additional Inexperienced Infantry Section for free.

NO TASTE FOR THE BAYONET

General Graziani undertook the military operation against the British with extreme reluctance, and this filtered down to his troops. To represent the lack of will of the Italians to die for *Il Duce* ('the leader'), when an Italian infantry unit suffers casualties in close combat, an equal number of models are immediately removed as casualties to represent Italians surrendering to their attackers. Combat then continues as normal, with the additional casualties unable to fight back (just like normal casualties) and counted towards the combat's resolution. If insufficient models are left to remove, simply remove what is left.

SCENARIOS

GENERAL SCENARIOS

O'Connor's main tactic was encirclement followed by an assault on the Italian defended positions. The following scenarios from the *Bolt Action* rulebook are ideal to represent this sort of attack. Note that the Italians will be the defenders in this type of action. Because of their lack of preparation, no Italian units may begin the game in hiding.

• Scenario 1: Envelopment (page 108)
• Scenario 3: Point Defence (page 112)
• Scenario 4: Hold Until Relieved (page 114)

Between attacks on the Italian defensive positions, the Italians would often send out strong patrols to probe for enemy movement in the desert. The following scenario is good at representing such forays. These encounters always happen in the day (so the Dawn/Dusk rule is not applicable).

• Scenario 2: Maximum Attrition (page 110)

SCENARIO 1: THE JAWS OF THE TRAP – THE BATTLE OF BEDA FOMM

With the British winning battle after battle, and penetrating deep into Libya, the Italian 10th Army was forced to retreat along the coast road. The 7th Armoured Division, with the 11th Hussars leading, swept across the desert to cut off the Italian retreat south of Benghazi at Beda Fomm. Meanwhile, the 6th Australian Division closed in, following along the road. Unless the Italians could break through the blocking British regiments, the Australians would threaten the rear of their column, and the entire army could be destroyed.

The following scenario is designed to recreate the first stage of this battle, though you can adapt it for use in any World War II theatre. A small force of blocking troops is trying to stop a much larger enemy army from breaking through before an outflanking force arrives to attack them in the rear.

Note that this battle takes place during the day.

FORCES

This scenario is designed to be played with equal points values on both sides. The following reinforced platoons should be used to represent the forces involved:

ITALIANS

War in Africa Reinforced Platoon (*Armies of Italy and the Axis*, page 31). Remember that the Operation *Compass* special rules apply, allowing, for example, free Inexperienced infantry sections to the Italians. Because mobility is essential for the Italians in this scenario, the Italian player can have as many (Inexperienced) trucks as required to carry his infantry, for free.

BRITISH & COMMONWEALTH

Operation *Compass* Reinforced Platoon (*Armies of Great Britain*, page 72).

SET-UP

TERRAIN

The table is set up as shown on the scenario map. One short edge, the north edge, is the Italian force's table edge. The opposite side is the British table edge. The 'western' long table edge represents the Mediterranean coastline.

The coast road (6" wide) runs along the centre of the table, from short edge to short edge. This stretch is quite poorly maintained, so a vehicle moving along it can only double its move rate on the D6 score of a 4+.

The rest of the table is desert. Refer to the section on Desert terrain on page 121.

DEPLOYMENT

The British player sets up no more than a third of his units (but no tanks) in the Blocking Force Set-Up Zone (anywhere from the British edge to 12" from the table middle line) – this is the British blocking force. The British player can place an obstacle (e.g. piled up crates and sandbags) in front of any infantry unit that is on or partly on the road – this represents the British roadblock. The rest of the British army is the Outflanking Force, in reserve. Note that in this game, the usual rules for Outflanking are not used – instead, see the special version of these rules below. The British side counts as being the defenders in this scenario.

The Italian player sets aside up to half of his units (rounding up) as his First Wave – this half cannot contain any tanks. The rest of his force is his Second Wave, and are in reserve. Both waves begin the game off-table. The Italian side counts as being the attackers in this scenario.

SPECIAL RULES

FIRST TURN

The battle begins. During Turn 1, the Italian player must move his entire first wave onto the table. These units can enter the table from any point on the attacker's table edge, and must be given either a *run* or *advance* order. Note that no order test is required to move units onto the table as part of the first wave.

OPERATION *COMPASS*/DESERT WARFARE

See the rules for Operation *Compass* (page 16) and Desert Warfare (page 121). Note that this scenario occurs at daytime.

DESERT FIGHTERS

All British units have, by now, had ample experience of desert combat by now, so have the Desert Fighters rule (see page 122).

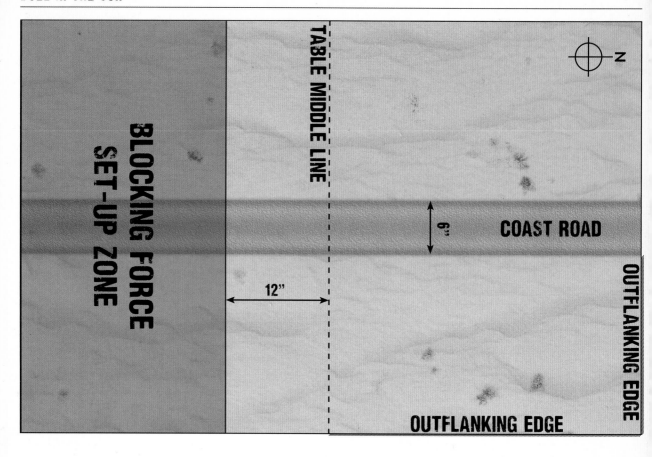

Map labels:
- TABLE MIDDLE LINE
- N
- BLOCKING FORCE SET-UP ZONE
- COAST ROAD
- 6"
- 12"
- OUTFLANKING EDGE
- OUTFLANKING EDGE

OUTFLANKING FORCE

When any unit in Reserve as part of the Outflanking Force is activated, they move on from any point along an Outflanking Edge, as shown on the map – that is, any point along a table edge east of the coast road between (and including) the Italian edge and the table middle line.

OBJECTIVE

The Italian player must try to move as many of his units as he can into the Blocking Force set-up zone or off the British edge. The British player must try to stop him. Note that in this scenario, Italian units are allowed to deliberately move off the table from the British edge to reach their objective.

GAME DURATION

Keep a count of how many turns have elapsed as the game is played. At the end of Turn 8, roll a die. On a result of 1, 2 or 3 the game ends, on a roll of 4, 5 or 6 play one further turn.

VICTORY!

At the end of the game, calculate which side has won by adding up victory points as follows. If one side scores at least 2 more victory points than the other then that side has won a clear victory. Otherwise the result is deemed too close to call and honours are shared – a draw!

The Italian player scores 1 victory point for every enemy unit destroyed. He also scores 2 victory points for each of his own units that is inside the Blocking Force set-up zone (even if only partially), and 3 victory points for each of his own units that has moved off the enemy table edge before the end of the game.

The British player scores 2 victory points for every enemy unit destroyed.

Italian Army light mortar team

SCENARIO 2: THE CAPTURE OF KUFRA

West of Italy's North African possessions were French colonies. At the fall of France in 1941, their governors had declared for the Vichy government, and so posed no threat to Mussolini. However, several French colonies in Africa swore loyalty to the Free French government in exile, headed by Charles de Gaulle in London.

The Free French in Chad, commanded by Lieutenant-Colonel Jean Colonna d'Ornano, targeted Italian positions at Kufra, Lybia, in January, crossing 400km of desert that had previously proved impassable to most vehicles. They were assisted by the British Long Range Desert Group (LRDG), a reconnaissance and raiding unit tasked with patrolling behind enemy lines to gain intelligence, comprising of 76 men in 26 vehicles adapted to desert conditions, led by Major Pat Clayton.

Kufra was key to the communications between Italian Libya and Italian East Africa – the sole lifeline for the Duke of Aorta's beleaguered Abyssinian forces. Vital to this link was the airport at Buma, guarded by the fort at El Tag.

Despite the death of D'Ornamo (replaced by Colonel Phillippe Leclerc) in an initial raid on 11 January, and the capture of Clayton by a Saharan patrol on 31 January and subsequent defeat of the LRDG, the Free French eventually besieged El Tag and forced the Italian garrison into surrender on 1 March.

The relatively small-scale nature of the Battle of Kufra and the derring-do of the British and Free French attackers makes this action an ideal subject for games of *Bolt Action*. Details on how to fight the battle using the *Bolt Action* rules are as follows.

FORCES

The following forces should be used:

ITALIANS

War in Africa Reinforced Platoon (*Armies of Italy and the Axis*, page 31), with the following exceptions:

- **HQ:** You can have 1 Forward Air Observer unit for free.
- **Infantry:** All Infantry sections must be Colonial troops. You cannot choose an Anti-tank rifle team or a Flamethrower team.
- **Artillery:** You can only choose either light artillery or a Breda 20mm AA gun.
- **Armoured Cars and Recce Vehicles:** You cannot choose a Sahariana.
- **Tanks, Self-Propelled Guns and Anti-Aircraft Vehicles:** You cannot choose any of these types of vehicle.
- **Transports and Tows:** You can only choose trucks. You can have as many (Regular) trucks as you need to transport your infantry, for free.

FREE FRENCH

Free French Reinforced Platoon – use the Defence of Vichy selector from page 36 of *Armies of France and the Allies*, except that the Army special rules on page 10–11 of the *Armies of France and the Allies* do not apply. Instead use the Vengeance special rule:

- **Vengeance:** Every unit that has one or more pin markers can make a test to lose one pin marker if there are any enemy within 12" immediately before an order is given to it. For example, a unit of infantry has two pin markers and there is an Italian unit within 12" – when the infantry are allocated an order they can test to lose one pin marker immediately before the order test is taken. Roll a die: on a roll of 4, 5 or 6 the test is passed and the unit loses one pin marker; on a 1, 2 or 3 the test is failed and the unit retains the pin markers it has. Once this has been done, continue to test to see if the unit obeys its order in the usual way, even if they have lost their last pin marker (in which case the Order test is taken without negative modifiers from pin markers).

LRDG

Behind Enemy Lines Reinforced Platoon (*Armies of Great Britain*, page 73).

Italian Army command squad

SCENARIOS

GENERAL SCENARIOS

The Capture of Kufra involved a series of separate encounters and raids, culminating in the siege of the fort of El Tag. The preliminary raid – the attack on the Italian airfield at Murzuk, has its own special scenario detailed below. Subsequent actions involved the Italians intercepting the LRDG *en route* to attack El Tag fort (which resulted in the LRDG being forced to retreat), and a similar interception against Leclerc's Free French, with the French victory paving the way for the siege itself.

The Maximum Attrition scenario (*Bolt Action* page 110) is ideal to represent the interceptions. The siege was a rather anti-climactic affair, with the inexperienced Italian commander surrendering the fort after a mere two weeks, so unless you want to simply set up your forces and leave them in situ for a fortnight, we don't recommend you re-enact it on the tabletop.

Note that all these battles take place by day.

SPECIAL RULES

DESERT WARFARE

This battle were fought in the desert. See the rules for Desert Warfare, on page 121.

DESERT FIGHTERS

All units involved in the battle were experienced in desert combat, so have the Desert Fighters special rule (see page 122).

A DARING RAID

The following scenario allows you to play out the daring daylight raid of the Free French and LRDG against the defenders of the Italian airfield at Murzuk. It can in fact be used to represent any similar raid in any other World War II theatre.

FORCES

This scenario is designed to be played with equal points values on both sides. Note that this scenario makes an excellent three-player game, with one person controlling one of each of the nationalities involved in the raid. In a three-player game, Lieutenant-Colonel d'Ornano leads the Free French, while Major Clayton leads the LRDG.

ITALIANS

War in Africa Reinforced Platoon (*Armies of Italy and the Axis*, page 31) – with the restrictions given on page 19 (Capture of Kufra Theatre Selectors). Note that the other rules for Operation *Compass* (like 'Eight million bayonets' and 'No taste for the bayonet') do not apply to this scenario.

LRDG

Behind Enemy Lines Reinforced Platoon (*Armies of Great Britain*, page 73) – must be led by a Major (Pat Clayton).

FREE FRENCH

Only eleven Free French participated in this attack. The Free French platoon consists of three units: Lieutenant-Colonel Jean Colonna d'Ornano (Veteran Officer with +5 Officer Morale Modifier), plus a five-man unit of *Groupe Franc* Veteran Infantry (may be upgraded with extra weapons, but not extra soldiers), and a five-men unit of Senegalese *Tirailleurs* Infantry (may be upgraded with extra weapons, but not extra soldiers).

A diversionary raid was attempted by French camel cavalry, but was driven off, and these troops had no effect on the outcome of the battle. If the player controlling the Free French wants to, he can purchase a unit of camelry (see page 13). However, there's a good chance that this unit might not make it to the battle (see later).

SET-UP

TERRAIN

Set up a mud-brick fort (about 12" square) and an airstrip within a delineated airfield (12" x 36") as shown on the map.

Place three Italian aircraft on the airstrip (any type will do, or you can use markers to represent them – in the actual battle the Allies were attempting to destroy Caproni bombers).

The rest of the battlefield is typical desert terrain (see page 121).

DEPLOYMENT

The Italian player sets up first, placing all his units inside the fort or within the airfield perimeter.

The Allied side can split its units into up to four waves. Each wave begins the game off-table. Before the game starts, the Allied side must secretly write down which table edge each wave will be moving onto the table from. Each wave must move on from a different table edge (otherwise it cannot move on at all – there's been a breakdown in communications).

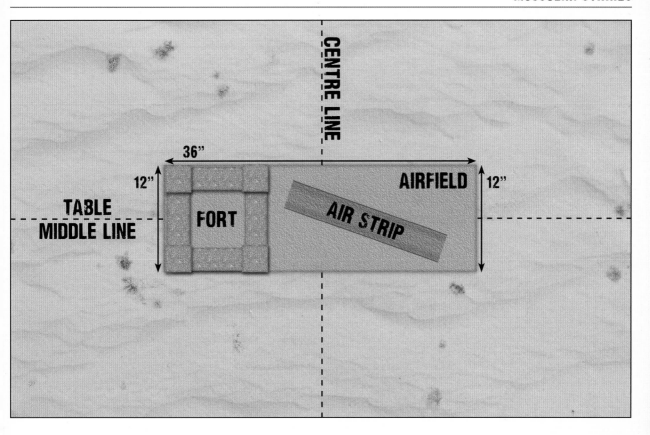

The camelry, if used, do not count as being in a wave, and are held in reserve separately.

SPECIAL RULES

FIRST TURN

During Turn 1, the Allied side must bring his first wave onto the table. These units can enter the table from any point on the designated table edge, and must be given either a *run* or *advance* order. Note that no order test is required to move units onto the table as part of the first wave.

If there are any troops in a second, third or fourth wave, all units in these waves count as Reserves.

DESERT WARFARE

See the rules for Desert Warfare, on page 121. Note that this scenario occurs at daytime. The attackers have managed to evade, capture or kill all enemy sentries and achieve complete surprise, so the Dust Trail special rule is not used in this scenario.

DESERT FIGHTERS

All units have the Desert Fighters rule (see page 122).

RESERVES

Reserve units can enter the table from any point on the table edge designated for their wave. Note that units in these waves can enter in any order – units in the third wave, for example, don't have to wait until all units in the second wave have entered the table.

A normal Outflanking Manoeuvre cannot be used in this scenario.

CAMELRY

If the French Camelry unit is successfully ordered onto the table, its controlling player nominates each table edge a number from 1 to 4 and rolls a D6. On a 1–4, if the player wants, the Camelry unit can be deployed as a Reserve on the table edge nominated as the same number. On a 5–6, the Camelry unit has been destroyed in a skirmish beyond the battlefield and cannot turn up (the order die drawn for the unit is discarded – note that the unit does not count as destroyed if it fails to turn up in this way).

OBJECTIVE

The Allied side must try to destroy as many aircraft as it can. The Italians must try to stop them.

An aircraft is destroyed if, at the end of any turn, any enemy unit is touching it (other than an empty transport vehicle). Empty transports cannot be used to destroy an aircraft, although a transport vehicle carrying troops can.

Mark a destroyed airplane with a suitable marker (such as cotton wool). Leave the model/marker where it is as it still counts for cover.

Note that the planes remain static throughout the game.

GAME DURATION

Keep a count of how many turns have elapsed as the game is played. At the end of Turn 6, roll a die. On a result of 1, 2 or 3 the game ends, on a roll of 4, 5 or 6 play one further turn.

ADDITIONAL UNITS

ITALY

LANCIA ANSALDO IZ AND IZM

The most numerous Italian armoured car to be produced during World War I, the Lancia Ansaldo IZ and IZM saw action in both World Wars as well as during the inter-war period. Ten Lancia IZ were produced in 1916. Characterised by its two-tier machine-gun turrets, the Lancia IZ's other most recognisable feature were the cutting rails designed to deal with barbed wire and similar obstacles prevalent on the battlefield of the Great War. Seeing the success of the IZ, the Italian army ordered 110 more, but after concerns about stability the top machine-gun turret was removed. The rear fighting compartment was equipped with an extra port for a third machine-gun, and a rack for a liaison bicycle. The resultant IZM became available in 1917. The two versions of the Lancia armoured car were used well guarding against Austrian incursions, playing an important part in the rearguard action covering the retreating Italian forces at Caporetto in 1917. Following the action at Caporetto, it wasn't uncommon to see Lancias in service with German and Austrian armies as spoils of war. During the 20s and 30s, the majority of IZMs were sent to East Africa and Libya as the Italians looked to protect their eastern colonies. The IZMs saw action during the Ethiopian Campaign in 1935, acting as reconnaissance units. The small *Corpo Truppe Volontarie Italia* also fought in the Spanish Civil War of 1936–38, supporting the Nationalists, although these all but obsolete armoured cars fell prey to the Russian BA-3 and BA-6 armoured cars. These completely outdated machines were still in service in Libya and other East African colonies when World War II broke out. Most fought in Eastern Africa where they met equally vintage British and Australian armoured cars, and were all but wiped out during the course of those actions. Some were deployed with Italian troops in police and anti-partisan operations in the Balkans, primarily in Yugoslavia. By November 1943, those that survived were captured and pressed into German service. Some were sent to the army of Hungary. Most were destroyed or captured in 1944 during the Yugoslavian uprising and Allied conquest of Italy.

Cost: 64pts (Inexperienced), 80pts (Regular), 96pts (Veteran)
Weapons: two turret-mounted MMGs
Damage Value: 7+ (armoured car)
Options:

* Add one hull-mounted, rear-facing MMG for +10pts.
* Add one MMG mounted in a second, independent turret for +5pts. This is the original IZ version, which also suffers the 'Too many turrets!' rule (see below) and cannot have the optional rear-mounted MMG.

Special Rules:

* Recce.
* Too many turrets! (IZ version only): Three MMGs mounted on two separate-targeting concentric turrets in such a crammed space led to space and stability problems. To represent this, it is always necessary to make an order test when issuing an Advance order, even if the vehicle is not pinned.

SELECTORS

The IZ and IZM are Armoured Cars for the purposes of the generic Reinforced Platoon selector from the *Bolt Action* rulebook and for all of the selectors of the *Armies of Italy* book, except for those on the Eastern Front.

VICTORY!

At the end of the game, calculate which side has won by adding up victory points as follows. If one side scores at least 2 more victory points than the other then that side has won a clear victory. Otherwise the result is deemed too close to call and honours are shared – a draw!

The Italian player scores 1 victory point for every enemy unit destroyed. He also scores 3 victory points for each undestroyed airplane on the airstrip.

The Allied side scores 1 victory point for every enemy unit destroyed. Also, 3 victory points are scored by the Allied side for each destroyed enemy airplane.

THEATRE SELECTORS

THE INDIAN ARMY

The British Indian army increased from over 200,000 men at the start of the war to 2.5 million by the end. A typical Indian division was commanded by British expatriate officers, with subordinate British and Indian officers serving side-by-side, and recruited from native Indians, with some British regiments attached to battalions. Indian divisions took part in all the main North African operations up to and including the Second Battle of Alamein, as well as the Battle of Monte Cassino and the Gothic Line in Italy. Two divisions, the 4th and 5th, were involved in the defence of British possessions in East Africa. Indian divisions also served with distinction in other theatres beyond the scope of this supplement, notably Burma. Field-Marshal Sir Claude Auchinleck, Commander-in-Chief of the Indian Army from 1942 stated that the British "couldn't have come through both wars if they hadn't had the Indian Army."

INDIAN DIVISION REINFORCED PLATOON

To field an Indian Division reinforced platoon, select your force as normal from the appropriate theatre selector from *Armies of Great Britain* (in this case the Operation *Compass* selector). In addition, you may trade all three of the British Army Special rules from pages 17 and 18 of the *Armies of Great Britain* for the following special rules:

- **Unsurpassed Bravery:** Churchill paid tribute to "the unsurpassed bravery of Indian soldiers and officers." To reflect this, whenever a unit of infantry or artillery fails a morale check and would otherwise be destroyed as a consequence, take the test again and apply this second result.
- **The Manpower of the Empire:** To represent the vast manpower available within the Indian subcontinent, the Indian force gets a free ten-man Regular infantry section (early war), armed with rifles. Any additional equipment for this section may be purchased as normal.

Sikh medium mortar team

GREECE AND CRETE

The Genz glider detachment landing southwest of Canea on the morning of 20 May 1941, by Howard Gerrard © Osprey Publishing

Mussolini's disastrous attack on Greece had drawn Britain into south-east Europe. In November 1940, in response to a call for help from General Metaxas, the Royal Air Force landed squadrons on Greek soil and British troops landed on Crete allowing the Greek garrisons there to shift to the Albanian front.

Hitler rightly feared that the British presence in Greece would allow the RAF to interfere in his plans for the Balkans. The Balkans were to be the bulwark for the southern flank of the battlefront in Hitler's planned invasion of the Soviet Union. The Romanians, under Marshal Ion Antonescu, were friendly to the Nazis, and would provide a vital source of manpower for the German army. Furthermore, Hitler's panzers, on which his Blitzkrieg of the East depended so much, needed the ready source of fuel from the oilfields of Ploesti, 56km north of Bucharest. British warplanes being in bombing range of Ploesti would prove a great threat to Hitler's plans – thus, he had to wrest Greece from Allied influence.

OPERATION *MARITA*

In April 1941, Greece was invaded by the German 12th Army, under *Generalfeldmarschall* Wilhelm List, marching from Bulgaria and Yugoslavia, via Hungary and Romania. All these countries, threatened by the Soviet sphere of influence, had developed anti-Communist regimes who proved willing allies to Germany. Stalin was deeply suspicious of German manoeuvres so close to his borders, but Hitler assured his 'ally' that he had no ulterior motive other than dislodging the British from Greece.

An unintended consequence of Hitler's build-up of forces on the Greek frontier during the first three months of 1941 was that Churchill ordered Wavell to abandon further advances into Libya, and to divert three divisions from North Africa to Greece. This force, about 60,000 strong, half of which consisted of Australians and New Zealanders, was nowhere near enough to match the German juggernaut massing against the beleaguered Greek defenders – already engaged with the Italians on the Albanian border. The British commander, General Sir 'Jumbo' Maitland Wilson, and his senior officers, did not share the War Office's over-optimistic view of the coming campaign, and had fully prepared contingency plans to defend the Peloponnese in the south once northern Greece was overrun by the Germans. But the British government had promised Greece military aid if necessary back in 1939, so the British forces tried at first to defend the entire Greek territory.

Wilson's force occupied the banks of the Aliakmon, facing Bulgaria. The 2nd New Zealand Division, commanded by Major General Bernard Freyberg, held the left flank, with the 6th Australian Division, already bloodied in Libya, on the right. The British 1st Armoured Division acted as a screening force in front. Their presence provided a much-needed morale boost to the Greek troops who defended the border alongside them.

On 26 March, the Italian navy was persuaded by the Germans to attack Admiral Cunningam's fleet at Cape Matapan, Crete, supported by X *Fliegerkorps* from Sicily. Battle was joined two days later, but the British had foreknowledge of the Axis battle plans thanks to Bletchley Park's Ultra intercepts, and Cunningham was fully prepared.

The Italian fleet was battered, with three heavy cruisers and two destroyers sunk. Although a victory for the Royal Navy, the attack masked the troop carriers transporting the Afrika Korps from southern Italy to Libya – the Italian ships had been sacrificed to ensure the safety of Rommel's troops.

Hitler's invasion of Greece was slightly delayed by a catastrophe in Yugoslavia, where the pro-Nazi regent was deposed and anti-German demonstrations swept through the streets of Belgrade. This resulted in Hitler ordering the Luftwaffe to devastate Belgrade from the air, causing countless thousands of civilian casualties. On 6 April, List's 12th Army swarmed into Greece. This was accompanied by a simultaneous assault by Germany and her Balkan allies on Yugoslavia, whose hastily mobilised defenders crumbled quickly before the combined onslaught of Luftwaffe and panzer attacks.

On 17 April, Yugoslavia surrendered, and her lands were divided up between her Axis-friendly neighbours. For the rest of the war, the country would be racked by guerrilla warfare as desperate Serbians fought against the occupiers.

In contrast, the Greeks put up stubborn resistance, until the German XVIII Mountain Corps broke through the line and seized the Greek city of Salonika. Meanwhile, the British carefully withdrew before the might of the German army, having to abandon tanks and vehicles not designed for mountain warfare. The RAF was outnumbered by the invaders' Messerschmitts, and could play little role in the battle. Contact between the British and Greek armies was soon lost as the British out-retreated the weary Greeks.

Wilson ordered a retreat to the Thermopylae Line. The 5th New Zealand Brigade made a valiant effort at emulating the famous stand of the Spartans here by holding out against the 2nd Panzer Division and the 6th Mountain Division for three days at the Vale of Tempe.

The Greek prime minister committed suicide on 18 April. He escaped witnessing the horrors of occupation, where 40,000 of his compatriots died. General Wavell gave the order to evacuate all his troops from the stricken country. Greece formally surrendered on 20 April. At dawn that day, German paratroopers landed south of the Corinth Canal in a bid to cut off the British and Commonwealth retreat, but were given short shrift by units of New Zealanders supported by a few light tanks of the 4th Hussars. Most of the Allied force managed to escape via the Peloponnese, extricated by the ships of the Royal Navy, the remaining few bombers of the RAF and a fleet of local ships. The loss of so much valuable war materiel, though, was hard to bear. In many ways, the British operation in Greece was

another Dunkirk – a brave defence against an overwhelming foe, a daring escapade in the face of utter defeat. Unlike at Dunkirk, the British generals had Ultra at their disposal, and knew exactly when it was the right time to withdraw, saving many of their troops from needless sacrifice. Despite defeat, the veterans of the Greek campaign lived to fight on, re-armed and re-equipped. However, this diversion of forces from North Africa, at exactly the time as Rommel's forces entered the fray, severely jeopardised all the gains won by the British in Libya.

OPERATION *MERCURY*

Most of the British troops, having survived dive-bombing Stukas and waves of Junkers 88 and Messerschmitts throughout their brief sea journey, disembarked at Crete. It was to this island that Hitler next turned his attention to. Crete would provide him with a secure airbase from where he could bomb the Egyptian port of Alexandria and the Suez Canal.

General der Flieger Kurt Student succeeded in persuading Hitler that he could take the island with an airborne force. The plan was codenamed Operation *Mercury*.

Wavell asked Major General Freyberg to conduct the defence of Crete with his New Zealanders. Unfortunately, Freyberg was convinced that the attack would come by sea,

Hidden amonst the ruins, the Germans patiently await the Allies

despite being given intelligence to the contrary, and his defences neglected to take into account a serious airborne invasion. Luckily, German intelligence also proved lacking, and they greatly underestimated the number of enemy defenders.

Throughout May, German air attacks against Crete focused on the British airfields and air defence. At dawn, on 20 May, following intense attacks from German fighter-bombers, the first wave of German troops came in on gliders, closely followed by the main force of paratroopers in Junkers transports. Freyberg had known they were coming, thanks to Ultra decrypts, but was still convinced that the air invasion would be accompanied by an amphibious assault. He refused to target his artillery against the landing zones, keeping them trained seawards to ward off a phantom fleet, and failed to commit his reserves on time, keeping them back for a wave of German troop transport ships that never materialised. Also, due to a shortage of wireless sets, the troops in the east of the island did not discover that the western parts were under attack until mid-afternoon.

Nevertheless, the Germans suffered severe casualties when they landed in areas where there were sufficient defenders. Many aircraft were shot down as they descended, and some units were dropped into the sea or injured by landing on dangerous ground. The Germans also faced the ire of the civilian population, who slaughtered paratroopers they caught alone or who got stuck in trees, and who were slaughtered in turn during the reprisals that followed after the island's eventual capture.

Crete's capital, Heraklion, was taken by the III Battalion, despite a fierce defence from Greek troops and local militia, but was recaptured when the York & Lancaster Regiment and Leicestershire Regiment counter-attacked.

As night fell, it was apparent that the German plan had gone awry. None of their primary objectives, including their main target, Maleme airfield, had been taken, and the paratroopers were constantly harassed by ambushes in the dark by Cretan irregulars. Many officers had been killed in the assault.

However, Freyberg, in continuing to ignore sound military intelligence, snatched defeat from the jaws of victory – he failed to unleash his reserves, still convinced that there were German troopships on the horizon. Indeed, a small German flotilla was running the gauntlet in the dark, attempting to bring much needed reinforcements and supplies to the paratroopers holed up on the island. The Royal Navy knew their exact position, again thanks to Ultra, and made short work of the boats – only one made it to shore. Freyberg watched this engagement from the horizon, and was convinced that Crete was now safe – a boon for the Germans on the island who still posed a serious threat.

The situation at Maleme was still in the balance. Lieutenant Colonel L.W. Andrew VC, leading the New Zealand 22nd Battalion, had throughout the day, denied the enemy the airfield from his vantage point known as Hill 107. By nightfall his men were exhausted, and Andrew repeatedly requested a counter-attack to secure the airfield, but was repeatedly ignored. He had no choice but to withdraw, leaving Maleme to the enemy, his men sacrificed to no avail. In response, General Student, directing events from his headquarters in Athens, ordered every available German reserve to be immediately dropped on Maleme.

A swift counter-attack from the Allies should have swept the Germans from Maleme, but Freyberg insisted that the 20th Battalion, poised to strike at 0100 hours, should not attack until its current position was taken over by the Australian battalion at Georgioupolis. Lacking transport, the Australians were delayed, and the 20th Battalion did not commence its attack, alongside the 28th (Maori) Battalion, for another two and a half hours. By this time, the enemy had securely reinforced Maleme, and the New Zealanders fought well into the next day, strafed continually by Messerschmitts when they lost the security of night at daybreak. They pulled back in the afternoon, ceding Maleme to the enemy. With the airfield tight in their grasp, the German build-up was relentless, as troop carrier after troop carrier landed and disgorged fresh troops onto Cretan soil.

At sea, too, the Germans began to get the upper hand, with two cruisers and three destroyers sunk by intensive air attack over two days, and two battleships and several more ships badly damaged.

With Maleme lost, Freyberg refused to commit his reserves in an all-or-nothing battle, but instead sounded the retreat. On 28 May, the defenders departed Crete from the port of Sphakia, evacuated once more by the Royal Navy. Many of the survivors perished during the voyage to Alexandria, hounded remorselessly by Stukas. The last ships left Crete on 1 June, forced to leave behind almost 10,000 men to be taken prisoner.

It had been a hard-won and very fortunate victory for the Axis. They had suffered 6,000 casualties, and almost 150 aircraft, and the Italian fleet had been badly mauled. Hitler lost any respect he had for an airborne invasion, and perhaps the bloody nose suffered by his forces attacking a small, well-defended island made him think twice about invading Malta. This British enclave in the eastern Mediterranean would soon prove invaluable in providing air support during the bitter fighting that was to come in North Africa and Italy.

FIGHTING THE BATTLE OF GREECE USING *BOLT ACTION*

The Battle of Greece offers Allied players the opportunity to play out scenarios where a smaller Allied force faces off against the juggernaut that is the German army in a hostile, highland landscape.

THEATRE SELECTORS

The following theatre selectors should be used to represent the forces involved in The Battle of Greece:

GREEKS

- Battle of Greece Reinforced Platoon (*Armies of France and the Allies*, page 94).

BRITISH & COMMONWEALTH

- Operation *Compass* Reinforced Platoon (*Armies of Great Britain*, page 72).

GERMANS

- 1941 – Operation *Barbarossa* Reinforced Platoon (*Armies of Germany*, page 73).

ITALIANS

- The Invasion of Greece Reinforced Platoon (*Armies of Italy and the Axis*, page 30) – The Italians were engaged with Greek forces along the Greek/Albanian border, so did not get into contact with the British Commonwealth forces in Greece.

THE BATTLE OF GREECE SPECIAL RULES

The following special rules are pertinent to battles fought in this campaign:

MULTINATIONAL FORCES

The British Commonwealth forces often fought alongside the Greeks in this theatre. Refer to the rules on page 120 if you want to field multinational forces.

NIGHT FIGHTING

Feel free to use the Night Attack rules for any games set during the battle of Greece. Alternatively, if both players agree, at the start of a battle before set-up, each player can roll a D6 and add the Officer Morale modifier of their commanding officer. If one player scores higher than the other, that player can decide to use the Night Fighting rules.

VASTLY OUTNUMBERED

Hitler threw his entire 12th Army at Greece, which vastly outnumbered the British Commonwealth force sent to help the Greek defenders, most of whom were tied up against the Italians along the Albanian border.

To represent this, if both players agree, any destroyed German Regular Infantry Section or Regular Tank worth no more than 250pts can be replaced as a German reserve at the end of the game turn during which it was destroyed. This reserve unit counts as a brand new unit, and the enemy gets victory points each time he destroys a unit (so if, say, a model tank gets 'destroyed', comes back as another reserve tank, and gets destroyed again, the opponent will score victory points twice for the same model).

GERMAN CONTROL OF THE SKIES

The Germans ruled the air during the battle of Greece. Throughout the Greek campaign, they flew 650 aircraft compared to the RAF's 80. To represent this, a German player benefits from the Control of the Skies rule on page 125.

SCENARIOS

GENERAL SCENARIOS

Any scenario from the *Bolt Action* rulebook is suitable for the kind of actions that took place during the battle of Greece. Note that Axis forces should normally be the attackers in battles fought in this theatre.

- Scenario 1: Envelopment (page 108)
- Scenario 2: Maximum Attrition (page 110)
- Scenario 3: Point Defence (page 112)
- Scenario 4: Hold Until Relieved (page 114)
- Scenario 5: Top Secret (page 115)
- Scenario 6: Demolition (page 116)

TERRAIN

Much of Greece, particularly in the north, consists of rugged, highland terrain. To represent the fact that many battles were fought along river valleys or through mountain passes, you might want to play scenarios lengthways along the tabletop, with players facing each across the short table edges. The long table edges are flanked by impassable mountains, so outflanking manoeuvres are not allowed.

Try to fill the tabletop with lots of rocky hills, escarpments, gullies, boulders, impassable rivers and the like, that will slow down infantry and impede the movement of other types of unit. These regions are sparsely inhabited, so few if any civilian buildings will be on the board.

The Greek borders were defended by many fortified bunkers, pillboxes and concrete emplacements, so in scenarios set during the initial part of the invasion, if an Allied player has a 'Defender's Set-up Zone', he can place one fortified building anywhere in this zone.

The few roads through the mountains were poorly maintained, so a vehicle moving along a road can only double its move rate on the D6 score of a 2+.

SCENARIO 3: DELAYING ACTION – THE BATTLE OF TEMPE GORGE

As the mighty 12th Army advanced through central Greece, the defeated Commonwealth forces retreated before them. On 18 April 1941, a small force of Australians and New Zealanders, were ordered to delay the Germans at Tempe Gorge, to give time for the main ANZAC force to escape. If they failed, the Germans would be able to cut off the ANZAC army and force it to surrender.

The holding force consisted merely of a two battalions of Australians equipped with small arms, mortars and anti-tank rifles, and a battalion of New Zealanders supported by artillery, yet they defended their positions for an entire day against determined German attacks. By dusk, the main ANZAC army had got to safety, and the holding force, battered but unbeaten, slipped away into the night, mission accomplished.

The following scenario is designed to recreate an action at the Battle of Tempe Gorge, though you can adapt it to represent a delaying action in any World War II theatre. Note that the battle takes place by day.

FORCES

In this scenario, the Germans have twice the number of requisition points as the ANZACs. The following reinforced platoons should be used to represent the forces involved:

BRITISH & COMMONWEALTH

Operation *Compass* Reinforced Platoon (*Armies of Great Britain*, page 72), with the following limits:

- **HQ:** The force cannot have any Forward Observers.
- **Infantry:** The force cannot have any Machine-Gun Teams.
- **Infantry only:** The force cannot be equipped with any vehicles.

GERMANS

1941 – Operation *Barbarossa* Reinforced Platoon (*Armies of Germany*, page 73). In addition, because they have air superiority, they can have a regular Air Force Forward Observer for free.

SET-UP

TERRAIN

Set up the terrain as shown on the map for this scenario.

The game is played lengthways along the table, with opponents facing each other across the short edges. The long table edges are flanked by impassable high ground, so outflanking manoeuvres are not allowed.

To represent the fact that the ANZACs have chosen the most advantageous spot available for their delaying action, the ANZAC player places all the terrain for this game.

The Pinios River stretches across the width of the table along the table's middle line.

Place a bridge in the exact centre of the table, crossing the river. This bridge has been blown by the New Zealanders, so counts as a section of river, but the rubble provides hard cover.

The ANZAC player must place up to two fords along the river, one on either side of the bridge. A ford cannot be placed within 12" of the bridge.

A road bisects the table, from the centre of the German table edge to the centre of the ANZAC edge, passing over the river at the bridge. The road is poorly maintained, so a vehicle moving along it can only double its move rate on the D6 score of a 4+.

Fill the tabletop with lots of rocky hills, escarpments, gullies, boulders and other highland terrain that impedes movement. However, don't place any impassable terrain on the table – the valley floor can be difficult to move across but not impossible. There are no buildings or woods on the battlefield, and no other water features other than the river.

DEPLOYMENT

The defender sets up all his units in the ANZAC set-up zone. These units can use the hidden set-up rules (*Bolt Action*, page 117).

The German player's units are not set up on the table at the start of the game. The German player must nominate up to half of the units in his force to form his first wave. Any units not included in the first wave are left in reserve.

SPECIAL RULES

PREPARATORY BOMBARDMENT
The German player rolls a die: on a 2+ a preparatory bombardment strikes the ANZAC positions (see *Bolt Action* page 118). On a result of 1, the barrage fails to materialise.

FIRST TURN
During Turn 1, the German player must move his entire first wave onto the table. These units can enter the table from any point on the attacker's table edge, and must be given either a *run* or *advance* order. Note that no order test is required to move units onto the table as part of the first wave.

THE RIVER PINIOS
Units attempting to cross the river use the Shallow Water rules on page 134. At the ruined bridge and the fords, treat the crossing point as rough ground, but impassable to wheeled vehicles. ANZAC units deployed within 3" of the river are allowed to use the Dug-in rules (page 124).

VASTLY OUTNUMBERED
See page 28.

GERMAN AIR SUPERIORITY
See page 28.

SHORT OF AMMO
The New Zealanders suffered a mauling a few days before the battle, and their artillery was short of shells. To represent this, during the game, the ANZAC player cannot use Indirect Fire and cannot shoot with an artillery unit that requires a 6 to hit its target – there is too little ammo to waste on anything other than a reasonably good shot over open sights.

EXTRA CHARGES
Immediately after the set-up phase, the ANZAC player can nominate one light mortar unit in his force to be commanded by Sgt Geoff Coyle. During the battle, Sgt Coyle's mortars resorted to using extra charges to improve their range. The unit can

increase the maximum range of its mortar by an extra 24". However, before firing the mortar, the ANZAC player must roll a D6. On a 1, the mortar explodes and the unit is removed as a casualty (the Germans score victory points for it as normal).

OBJECTIVE

The German player must try to move as many of his units as he can into the ANZAC set-up zone or off the opposing side's table edge. The ANZAC player must try to stop him. Note that in this scenario, attacking units are allowed to deliberately move off the table from the defender's table edge to reach their objective.

GAME DURATION

Keep a count of how many turns have elapsed as the game is played. At the end of Turn 7, roll a die. On a result of 1, 2 or 3 the game ends, on a roll of 4, 5 or 6 play one further turn.

VICTORY!

At the end of the game, calculate which side has won by adding up victory points as follows. If one side scores at least 2 more victory points than the other then that side has won a clear victory. Otherwise the result is deemed too close to call and honours are shared – a draw!

The German player scores 1 victory point for every enemy unit destroyed. He also scores 1 victory point for each of his own units that is inside the ANZAC set-up zone (even if only partially), and 3 victory points for each of his own units that has moved off the enemy table edge before the end of the game.

The ANZAC player scores 4 victory points for every enemy unit destroyed.

FIGHTING THE BATTLE OF CRETE USING *BOLT ACTION*

Surrounded by sea, the New Zealanders defending Crete were safe from invasion by land, but experienced the first ever large-scale paratrooper drop. Use the following rules to represent actions fought on the island.

THEATRE SELECTORS

The following theatre selectors should be used to represent the forces involved in the battle of Greece:

GREEKS

- Battle of Greece Reinforced Platoon (*Armies of France and the Allies*, page 94), except that the platoons cannot include any vehicles, nor medium and heavy field artillery.

BRITISH & COMMONWEALTH

- Operation *Compass* Reinforced Platoon (*Armies of Great Britain*, page 72), except that the only Tanks available are Matilda II and Light Tank Mark VIB.

GERMANS

- Operation *Mercury* Reinforced Platoon (*Armies of Germany*, page 78).
- *Fallschirmjäger* Reinforced Platoon (*page 36*).

THE BATTLE OF CRETE SPECIAL RULES

The following special rules are pertinent to battles fought in this campaign:

MULTINATIONAL FORCES

Greeks and British Commonwealth forces fought together on Crete. Refer to the rules on page 120 if you want to field multinational forces.

NIGHT FIGHTING

Feel free to use the Night Attack rules for any games set during the battle of Crete. Alternatively, if both players agree, at the start of a battle before set-up, each player can roll a D6 and add the Officer Morale modifier of their commanding officer. If one player scores higher than the other, that player can decide to use the Night Fighting rules.

GERMAN CONTROL OF THE SKIES

Before invading Crete, the Germans bombed the island with devastating raids that forced the RAF to move its planes to Alexandria, Egypt, winning the Luftwaffe control of the Cretan skies. To represent this, a German player benefits from the Control of the Skies rule on page 125.

AIRBORNE INVASION

If you want to play out the German airborne assault that initiated Operation *Mercury*, the players can alternatively agree that the German player will field either Airborne Platoons (page 126) using the Combat Jump rules (page 126), and/or Glider Landing Platoons (page 127) using the Glider Landing rules (see page 127).

ENIGMA CODE BROKEN

The battle of Crete was the first time that Ultra provided significant military intelligence for the Allies. For battles fought in this theatre (and indeed all battles described in the rest of this book) feel free to use the Ultra special rule:

- **Ultra:** Allied forces can re-roll the dice for initial set-up.

CRETAN RESISTANCE

For the first time in the war, the Germans faced a mass popular uprising in response to their invasion, and during the Battle of Crete, isolated paratroopers were often mobbed and hacked to death by enraged civilians.

To represent this situation, use the following rules in any battle fought on Crete except ones using the Combat Jump rules (see page 126). Before set-up, the German player must remove D6–3 infantry models of his choice from his force. These unlucky soldiers have fallen victim to civilian ambushes before the battle.

SCENARIOS

GENERAL SCENARIOS

The first day of the invasion should involve German Airborne Platoons or Glider Landing Platoons facing New Zealand or Greek forces. The following scenarios can represent actions fought during this initial stage, with the Germans automatically being the attackers:

- Scenario 1: Envelopment (page 108)
- Scenario 2: Maximum Attrition (page 110)
- Scenario 3: Point Defence (page 112)
- Scenario 4: Hold Until Relieved (page 114)

The second day should focus on the attack on Maleme airfield. The Maleme Airfield scenario (page 33) can be used to represent this attack, as well as attempts to capture smaller airfields on Crete. Subsequently, on the same day and the following day, attempts were made by the New Zealanders to recapture Maleme – Scenario 4 is ideal to represent these counter-attacks, with the German paratroopers as the defenders.

During the following week, the Germans stepped up their attacks, reinforced by more dropped paratroopers. The Allies were forced to withdraw, retreating southward across Crete. The Maximum Attrition scenario is ideal for representing this fighting withdrawal.

At one point, a German force blocked the retreat of a New Zealand force, which included the 28th Maori Battalion. The New Zealanders' attempts to clear the Germans can be represented by the Envelopment scenario, with the New Zealanders as the attackers.

At this stage of the battle, the Germans landed transports on Crete, up until then valiantly held at bay by the Royal Navy. The Italians also landed troops, but by then the New Zealanders were in the process of evacuating the island, and the Italian advance was unopposed.

Just before Crete fell to the Axis forces, a detachment of 800 men from No 7 and No 8 Commandos landed on the island tasked with performing rearguard actions to delay the German advance. This is a great way of involving a Raiders Reinforced Platoon in the fight (see *Armies of Great Britain*, page 69). Their actions can be represented by any of the *Bolt Action* scenarios, and can take place at night if the Commandos player wishes (see the Night Fighting rules on page 129).

TERRAIN

Inland, Crete's geography is similar to that of mainland Greece – difficult, mountainous territory. Refer to the section on Greek terrain, on page 28.

On the coast, the terrain is hilly rather than mountainous, and dotted with villages surrounded by agricultural land such as vineyards, olive groves and fruit orchards. The main aim of the Germans was to seize control of the largest Cretan towns on the north coast, Chania, Rethymno and Heraklion, and the Allied airfields. An airstrip with a control tower can make an impressive battlefield objective for an Allied force to defend.

Matilda II

SCENARIO 4: MALEME AIRFIELD

The airfield at Maleme is a vital objective for the Germans. If they can secure it, they will have obtained a foothold on the coast of northern Crete, and will quickly be able to use it to reinforce their positions with troops and materiel flown in on the Junkers JU52 transport aircraft waiting in the wings. The New Zealanders deployed at the airfield must defend it at all costs.

The following scenario is designed to recreate the German attempt to capture Maleme airfield, though you can adapt it for use in any World War II theatre.

FORCES

This scenario is designed to be played with equal points values on both sides. The following reinforced platoons should be used to represent the forces involved.

BRITISH & COMMONWEALTH

Operation *Compass* Reinforced Platoon (*Armies of Great Britain*, page 72) to represent the New Zealand forces fighting for the airfield, you must field at least one Maori Infantry

Section (see page 35) and the only vehicle you can field is a single Matilda II. Also, you cannot have any Forward Observers in your force.

GERMANS

Operation *Mercury* Reinforced Platoon (*Armies of Germany*, page 78) and/or *Fallschirmjäger* Reinforced Platoon (page 36). The Germans enjoy total air superiority, so have one Veteran Air Force Forward Observer for free.

SET-UP

TERRAIN

Set up the terrain as shown on the scenario map. There's a bridge in the exact centre of the table, crossing the Tavronitis River. A road crosses the table across it width – the road is well-maintained here, so the usual rules for roads apply.

The river counts as Shallow Water (see page 134). However, the controller of any tracked vehicle crossing the river must stop moving it when it is exactly halfway across and roll a D6 – on a 1

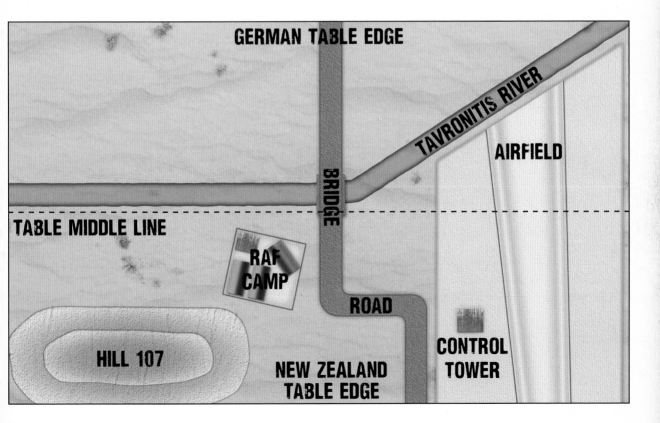

LEGENDS OF BRITAIN & THE COMMONWEALTH

CAPTAIN CHARLES UPHAM

Charles Upham was a soldier from New Zealand who fought valiantly in Greece, Crete and North Africa, becoming the only combat soldier (as opposed to medical staff) to earn the Victoria Cross twice, making him the most highly decorated soldier in the Commonwealth forces. He was exceptional at leading his men in furious assaults against strongly defended positions, where he would be always at the front, taking out one machine gun post after another with a well-placed hand grenade.

Cost: 200pts (Veteran)
Team: 1 officer and up to 2 other men
Weapons:

- Submachine gun, pistol or rifle, as depicted on the models

Options:

- Upham may be accompanied by up to 2 men at a cost of +13pts per man (Veteran)

Special Rules:

- Lead by example: Upham's Morale bonus is +4 and the range of his ability is 12".
- Master of close quarters: To represent his masterful use of grenades, his unit always attacks first when charging into close quarters, even if the enemy is in cover. In addition, Upham himself roll four dice for his close quarter attacks against infantry and artillery units, and his attacks have a Pen value of +1!

the vehicle hits a boulder and is stranded mid-stream (it counts as destroyed). On a 2–6, the vehicle can continue moving.

The RAF camp can be represented by a collection of Nissen huts or similar small, flimsy buildings.

The airfield can be represented by an airstrip (counts as a road) surrounded by a collection of small buildings and a control tower.

The hill represents Hill 107, and allows considerable field of fire across the battlefield. It has two tiers.

The table edge adjacent to the airfield represents the Cretan coastline.

The terrain on the German side of the river is a flat coastal plain, dotted with a few civilian buildings, but otherwise featureless.

DEPLOYMENT

First, the German player places an objective marker in the centre of the RAF camp, anywhere adjacent to the airfield control tower and anywhere on the second tier of Hill 107. Objective markers can be any size up to 3" in diameter.

He then places a *Fallschirmjäger* Squad anywhere in the airfield area on the German side of the table, up to 6" from the table's middle line. This represents German troops that have already got a foothold on the airfield.

The New Zealand player then deploys up to half of his units anywhere on his side of the table, up to the table's middle line, as long as none of his models are within 12" of an enemy model. Any of his units not deployed are in reserve. His Matilda tank, if present, **must** be kept in reserve.

The German player now deploys at least half of his units up to 6" from his table edge. Any of his units not deployed are in reserve.

SPECIAL RULES

PREPARATORY BOMBARDMENT

The German player enjoys air superiority, and the New Zealanders are pounded by bombing raids before the battle starts. To represent this, a preparatory bombardment automatically strikes the New Zealand positions (see *Bolt Action* page 118).

FIRST TURN

The battle begins.

HIDDEN SET-UP

The German unit set up in the airfield, and any New Zealand units deployed at the start of the game can be hidden at the start of the game (see *Bolt Action*, page 117).

DUG-IN

The German unit set up in the airfield, and any New Zealand units deployed at the start of the game can be Dug-in at the start of the game (see the Dug-in rules, page 124).

NEW ZEALAND RESERVES

New Zealand reserves can arrive from any point along the New Zealand table edge. However, the New Zealanders have been cut off from telephone contact with their HQ, and find it difficult to communicate with their reserves. New Zealand units moving from reserve require an order check with a –3 penalty instead of –1. However, the New Zealand commander does have a Matilda tank within easy reach of the battlefield, and any order check required to bring this on is at –1 as normal.

New Zealand reserves are not allowed to use outflanking manoeuvres.

GERMAN RESERVES

German reserves can move on from any point on the German table edge. They can perform an outflanking manoeuvre along the coastline edge of the table, representing their troops advancing on the battlefield from the beaches, but cannot outflank from the other edge of the table.

HOUNDED BY MESSERSCHMITTS

The Luftwaffe strafed and bombed the New Zealanders relentlessly throughout the battle. A German Forward Air Observer unit can call an Air Strike twice instead of once per game. Resolve the first air strike as normal. Then, in a subsequent turn, the FAO may call a second.

AMMUNITION LOW

By the end of the battle, ammo was running low on the New Zealand side. On Turn 6, the New Zealand player must roll a D6 before he shoots with an artillery unit – he can only fire with it if he scores a 4+. If there is a Turn 7, he needs a 6.

ENIGMA CODE BROKEN

Although Ultra is providing important information to the Allies during the Cretan campaign, particularly concerning enemy Naval movements, there is no intelligence relevant to this battle.

CRETAN RESISTANCE

The Germans may have experienced the wrath of the Cretan resistance before the battle. See the rules on page 32.

OBJECTIVE

The German player must try to capture the three objective markers – his opponent must try to stop him.

GAME DURATION

Keep a count of how many turns have elapsed as the game is played. At the end of Turn 6, roll a die. On a result of 1, 2 or 3 the game ends, on a roll of 4, 5 or 6 play one further turn.

VICTORY!

At the end of the game, calculate which side has won as follows:

If the Germans control two or three objectives, they win the game. If they hold one objective, the German player rolls a D6. On a 1–3, the game is a draw. On a 4+, due to a lack of communications with their HQ, the New Zealand commander believes the battle is lost and orders a withdrawal (the Germans win). If the Germans hold no objectives then the New Zealanders win.

All objectives are held by the New Zealand player at the start of the game regardless of where his troops are positioned. If an objective changes hands during the game then it remains under the control of that side until it is taken back.

To capture an objective there must be a model from one of your infantry or artillery units within 3" of the objective at the end of the turn, and there must be no enemy infantry or field artillery models within 3" of it.

ADDITIONAL UNITS

BRITAIN & THE COMMONWEALTH

MAORI INFANTRY SECTION

"Give me the Maori Battalion and I will conquer the world." – Rommel.

The Australian and New Zealand Army Corps (ANZAC) was originally formed in Egypt during World War I and famously saw action in the Battle of Gallipoli. The name was reintroduced in April 1941 when the Australian I Corps and the New Zealand 2nd Division were merged under the same command after being deployed in Greece. The name ANZAC corps ceased to be used after the force evacuated Greece towards the end of April. Stemming from their brutal experiences at Gallipoli during World War I, the ANZACs had a reputation for displaying strength and bravery when faced with adversity. They carried this reputation with them into the World War II. The 28th (Maori) Battalion (or simply the Maori Battalion) was raised in 1940 as part of the Second New Zealand Expeditionary Force, following pressure on the New Zealand government from Maori MPs. Fighting in the Greek, North African and Italian theatres, the Maoris soon gained a reputation as formidable fighters among allies and enemies alike. Throughout the war, the Maoris displayed the fighting spirit of their proud warrior ancestors, and the 28th became the most decorated New Zealand battalion of the conflict.

To represent a Maori infantry section, first pick a Regular or Veteran Infantry section (either early, mid- or late-war) from pages 22–24 of *Armies of Great Britain*. Then, upgrade the unit at a cost of +1pt per man – this confers to the unit the Formidable Fighters rule below.

- **Formidable Fighters:** The Maori do not benefit from the National characteristic you have chosen for the army. Instead, they always have the following three National characteristics: *Blood curdling charge*, *Up and 'at 'em*, and *Tough as boots*.

SELECTORS

The Maori Infantry Section is an Infantry squad for the purposes of the generic Reinforced Platoon selector from the *Bolt Action* rulebook. It is also an Infantry squad for any theatre selectors of the *Armies of Great Britain* book set in North Africa after May 1941 or in Italy.

THEATRE SELECTORS

GERMAN FALLSCHIRMJÄGER

FALLSCHIRMJÄGER REINFORCED PLATOON

1 *Fallschirmjäger* Officer – Lieutenant or 2nd Lieutenant
2 *Fallschirmjäger* squads

Plus:

Headquarters

0–1 *Fallschirmjäger* Captain or Major
0–1 *Fallschirmjäger* Medic Team
0–1 *Fallschirmjäger* Forward Observer (Air Observer only)

Infantry

0–4 Infantry Sections: *Fallschirmjäger* squads (early or late war, as appropriate)
0–1 *Fallschirmjäger* Machine gun team
0–1 *Fallschirmjäger* Medium Mortar team **OR** 2 x light *Fallschirmjäger* Light Mortar teams
0–2 *Fallschirmjäger* Anti-tank team: anti-tank rifle team, *panzerschreck* team (late war only)
0–1 *Fallschirmjäger* Sniper team
0–1 *Fallschirmjäger* Flamethrower team

Artillery

0–1 gun from:
Anti-Tank Gun: *Panzerbuchse* 41, Pak 36
Field Artillery: light artillery, LG40, LG40/1

Armoured Cars

None

Tanks, Tank Destroyers, Self-propelled Artillery and Anti-aircraft Vehicles

None

Transports and Tows

No transports
0–1 Tow from: Kettenkrad

SPECIAL RULES

Any specialists who were attached to the *Fallschirmjäger* had to meet the elite unit's exacting training and physical requirements. All units in this selector **must** be taken as Veteran, if there is a choice. In addition, all infantry and artillery units (including *Fallschirmjäger* squads) **must** spend an extra +1pt per man in the unit, giving them the 'Stubborn' special rule:

* **Stubborn:** If a Stubborn unit is forced to take a Morale check, they always use their full Morale value, ignoring any pin markers (remember that Order Tests are not Morale Checks!).

DUEL IN THE DESERT

The 'Trento' Division strongpoint at El Alamein, by Steve Noon © Osprey Publishing Ltd. Taken from Warrior 169: Italian Soldier in North Africa 1941–43.

As in Greece, Hitler was forced to send troops to North Africa to counter the inadequacy of Mussolini's fighting forces. Germany could ill afford to see Italy's fascist government overthrown by internal strife, and to avoid this, Mussolini's weak military power would have to be strengthened by German might.

OPERATION *SUNFLOWER*

On 12 February 1941, *Generalleutnant* Rommel and the first elements of his *Deutsches Afrika Korps* – the 5th Light Division, arrived in Tripoli. The entirety of *X Fliergerkorps* would be stationed in Sicily to provide air support to Rommel's troops, harass enemy shipping in the Mediterranean, and pound the British airfields at Malta, that Mediterranean rock that proved such a thorn in the side of Axis operations in the region.

The bulk of the 5th Light Division, currently stationed in Sicily, would not be ready for action until early April, so for now Rommel would have to depend on his Italian allies to secure Libya against further British encroachment. Rommel decreed that the front would be held at Sirte until he had consolidated his German forces. Although Rommel was nominally under the leadership of the Italians, in reality he executed full command. Mussolini and his generals had no choice. They were painfully aware that they had become junior partners in the war.

On the British front, the 2nd Armoured Division and the 9th Australian Division now held the line, replacing the veterans of Operation *Compass* (the 7th Armoured Division which had returned to Cairo for much-needed repairs, and the 6th Australian Division which had been shipped to Greece).

Rommel recognised the imperative of an immediate strike against the British. By the end of March, he had 25,000 German troops at his disposal, professionally armed and equipped, unlike his battered Italian allies who suffered an acute shortage of motor transport, and whose morale was shaken by their recent defeats. Rommel had begun to test the resolve of the British by skirmishing along the front, but Berlin denied his requests for reinforcements – the preparations for Operation *Barbarossa* – the invasion of the Soviet Union, eclipsed the conflict in North Africa. Rommel was ordered not to begin his push into Egypt until the defeat of the Soviets, which was optimistically predicted by the German top brass for well before the end of the year.

On 3 April, Rommel ordered his army into Cyrenaica, and sent the Italian Brescia Division to attack Benghazi. The man who had recently replaced O'Connor as commander of the British forces in Libya was Lieutenant General Philip Neame, and his inexperience soon became apparent as he handed Benghazi over without a fight. The already understrength 2nd Armoured Division lost all its tanks to mechanical failure and fuel shortages during the retreat. To make matters even worse for the British, Rommel's 5th Light Division seized the coastal road to Tobruk, cutting the defenders off from the rest of the British force. Disaster piled upon disaster, as General Neame, accompanied by O'Connor who had returned as his advisor, were taken prisoner by a German night patrol on 7 April when their driver took a wrong turning. From 6–8 April, the 3rd Indian Motor Brigade delayed Rommel's advance at Mechili, and although their stand bought time for the 9th Australian Division to reach Tobruk and build up its defences, the Germans captured their commander – Major General Gambier Perry, and his staff, along with a hoard of vital supplies.

The Desert Fox on the prowl.

German troops, Cyrenaica and Western Egypt 1941 (L–R): Oberschütze, Maschinengewehrbataillon 2, Tobruk; Unteroffizier, Pionierbataillon (mot.) 900, Fort Capuzzo; Schütze, Panzerjägerabteilung 33, Halfaya Pass, by Stephen Andrew © Osprey Publishing Ltd. Taken from Men-at-Arms 316: The German Army 1939–45 (2).

THE SIEGE OF TOBRUK

Rommel now turned his sights on Tobruk, convinced that the port would soon fall. But the 9th Australian Division would not give him his prize without a stiff fight. British officers regarded the Australian defenders with disdain as an ill-disciplined rabble, but instead they proved formidable and courageous fighters, led by Major General Leslie Morshead, known as 'Ming the Merciless' to his men due to his strict and demanding style of leadership.

The German assault on Tobruk began on the night of 13 April. Despite heavy losses, Rommel threw more of his men at the defences, but these again were hurled back by the rifle fire, anti-tank guns and strong artillery of the tenacious defenders. While this attack was taking place, Rommel sent several units against the Egyptian border, almost 100 miles away, where they were met with resistance by the 22nd Guards Brigade. Rommel quickly gained a reputation as a commander who could be ruthless with the lives of his troops – he dismissed *Generalmajor* Streich of the 5th Light Division for being overly protective of the men under his command. Rommel seemed to be everywhere at once, directing his men from the thick of fighting, racing between his scattered troops, often in his own personal reconnaissance plane.

On 30 April, reinforced by the 15th Panzer Division, Rommel attacked Tobruk again, and again suffered heavy losses, particularly among his tanks. By this time, ammunition was beginning to run low among the Axis forces. Just as had happened to the British following their initial successes with Operation *Compass*, the Axis forces were in danger of overstretching themselves. Both sides faced immense problems with supplying their troops in the desert from their base of operations. Between Tripoli and the front at Tobruk was a distance by road of almost 1,200km; from Cairo to Tobruk, 800km. Shipping across the Mediterranean was harried by attacks from enemy navies (particularly submarines) and air forces. Meanwhile, the land that both sides had to traverse was bleak, inhospitable desert, with few settled areas, which provided very little opportunity to forage.

Rommel's advantage was that the British forces were still reeling from their defeat in Greece. Coupled with the loss of the 2nd Armoured Division's tanks, the British feared the German commander's superiority in armour. This was offset by Operation *Tiger*, which managed to ship almost 300 Crusader tanks and over 50 Hurricanes by convoy through the Mediterranean in early May, with the loss of only a single transport. Before these reinforcements arrived, Wavell launched Operation *Brevity* on 15 May, in a combined attack by British and Indian troops, but the attackers were swiftly outflanked by Rommel, and pushed back beyond the Halfaya Pass, just within the Egyptian border.

Undeterred, and bolstered by the arrival of the new tanks, the British mounted another offensive on 15 June – Operation *Battleaxe*. Again the British enjoyed early successes, retaking Halfaya Pass, but again they were soon pushed back when Rommel's panzers once more outflanked them. The Afrika Korps suffered heavy casualties, but the British lost more tanks and aircraft, which were much more difficult to replace than men. While Rommel was promoted by a delighted Hitler, Wavell was replaced by General Sir Claude Auchinleck, whom Churchill hoped would instil a more aggressive fighting spirit in the British army of North Africa.

The intense heat of the North African summer put paid to any intentions that the generals of either side had of offensive action. In their trenches, plagued by flies and sand-fleas, the infantry from both sides suffered from a lack of sufficient water. By day they scorched, by night they froze. Military action was reduced to a few skirmishes along the Libyan border. Meanwhile the Axis forces continued to batter at Tobruk with artillery and bombing raids. Throughout the summer of 1941, the British 70th Division grimly held on to the port, reinforced by an Australian brigade, a Czech battalion and a Polish brigade. They were supplied the bare essentials by the Royal Navy, braving the heavily shelled harbour. In contrast, Rommel's supply line from Europe was constantly harassed by Royal Navy submarines and RAF raiders based in Malta, and many Axis ships ended at the bottom of the Mediterranean, including several troop transports bearing reinforcements.

8th Army 2-pdr anti-tank gun

CODE OF THE DESERT

An unwritten code of honour existed among the men who fought in the desert campaigns (that is until an officer of the British Indian Army wrote it down):

- Your chief concern is not to endanger your comrade.
- Because of the risk that you may bring him, you do not light fires after sunset.
- You do not use his slit trench at any time.
- Neither do you park your vehicle near the hole in the ground in which he lives.
- You do not borrow from him, and particularly you do not borrow those precious fluids – water and petrol.
- You do not give him compass bearings which you have not tested and of which you are not sure.
- You do not leave any mess behind that will breed flies.
- You do not ask him to convey your messages, your gear, or yourself unless it is his job to do so.

- You do not drink deeply of any man's bottles, for they may not be replenished. You make sure that he has many before you accept his cigarettes.
- You do not ask information beyond your job, for idle talk kills men.
- You do not grouse unduly, except concerning the folly of your own commanders. This is allowable. You criticise no other man's commanders.
- Of those things which you do, the first is to be hospitable and the second is to be courteous… there is time to be helpful to those who share your adventure. A cup of tea, therefore, is proffered to all comers…
- This code is the sum of fellowship in the desert. It knows no rank or any exception.

OPERATION *CRUSADER*

The stalemate continued until autumn. With the weather becoming less severe, it became a matter of which side would launch an offensive first. The British took the initiative. On 18 November, a newly formed Allied force, the British 8th Army, led by Lieutenant General Sir Alan Cunningham, mobilised Operation *Crusader* in a bid to break the siege of Tobruk. Crossing the Libyan frontier at night under radio silence, and hidden by sandstorms, Cunningham sprung his surprise attack.

With 300 cruiser tanks, 300 American Stuart light tanks, and over 100 Valentines and Matildas, the British stormed into Libya, the ground troops supported by over 500 aircraft. XXX Corps, with the bulk of the armour, attacked north-westwards with the intention of defeating the panzer divisions and smashing the enemy encircling Tobruk. The 7th Armoured Division thrust towards Sidi Rezegh on the high ground south-east of Tobruk, swiftly capturing the airfield and 19 German aircraft. However, on its left flank, the division was mauled by the Italian Ariete Armoured Division, and on its right attacked by elements of the 15th and 21st Panzer Divisions, advancing from the Via Balbia coast road. Had the German tanks not been hampered by shortfalls of fuel, the destruction they wrought would have been even more devastating.

General Cunningham ordered the defenders of Tobruk to break out on 21 November, a premature command given that the threat of the enemy panzers had not yet been neutralised. The besieged forces suffered heavy casualties, as did the units of the 7th Armoured Division supporting them – their tanks were decimated by fire from German 88mm guns, and attacked from the rear by panzers.

Cunningham now advanced XIII Corps north behind the Italian forces guarding the Libyan border, with the intention of engaging German positions at Halfaya Pass and Sollum near the coast. The New Zealand Division, veterans of Crete led by General Freyberg, and 7th Indian Division made good headway. At the same time, Cunningham again ordered the forces in Tobruk to attempt another breakout, but the 7th Armoured Brigade and 22nd Armoured Brigade, now both reduced to a handful of tanks, were forced back to the defensive line held by the 5th South African Brigade, south of Sidi Rezegh. On 23 November, Rommel encircled this force, wiping out most of the South Africans, but not before the Allied brigades had destroyed over 70 of his panzers – a heavy toll. The following morning, in a desperate bid for a swift victory, Rommel raced to the Egyptian

Crusader cruiser tank

Commonwealth QF 25-pdr crews prepare for action

frontier, personally leading the 21st Panzer Division, hoping to completely encircle and destroy the entire 8th Army. However, Rommel's position in this forward force meant that he could not coordinate properly with the rest of his army. On 26 November, the New Zealand Division took the airfields at Sidi Rezegh and at Kambut, leaving Rommel with no forward Luftwaffe bases and decreased air support. When Rommel was forced to retreat from the frontier in response to this reversal, his panzers were engaged by Hurricanes, which could now attack with impunity.

Now under orders from their new commander, Major General Neil Ritchie, who replaced the mentally exhausted Cunningham, the 8th Army continued its westwards attack. On 8 December, bereft of reinforcements and replacement materiel, Rommel abandoned the siege of Tobruk and, by early January 1942, retreated his forces to the line where he had begun his offensives at the start of 1941. Operation *Crusader* had been a success, and Tobruk, defiantly, remained in British hands.

OPERATION *THESEUS*

On the same day as Rommel initiated his withdrawal, America was reeling from the shock of the Japanese attack on Pearl Harbor. In solidarity with his Japanese allies, Germany declared war on America on 11 December. This drastically changed the situation in North Africa. Hitler believed that he had to shatter British morale before the Americans entered the war properly – he was convinced that the utter destruction of the 8th Army would achieve this. In addition, the capture of Egypt and the Suez Canal would mean that the Japanese could advance westwards into the Indian Ocean, and the pearl of the British Empire – India – would be seriously threatened from two sides. And so, at last, Rommel began receiving the support and resources from Berlin that he had long been petitioning for.

Rommel initiated his planned invasion of Egypt, codenamed Operation *Theseus*, with an outflanking manoeuvre against the British-held Gazala Line, which stretched from Gazala on the coast to Bir Hakheim, a desert outpost manned by the 1st

Free French Brigade of General Marie-Pierre Koenig. When he had defeated these defences, Rommel would march on Tobruk once more. Without this port, the vast distance between the Axis base at Tripoli and Egypt made supplying Rommel's invading army incredibly difficult.

The invasion began on 26 May with Italian infantry divisions attacking enemy positions in the north of the Gazala Line as a diversion. To the south, the 10,000 vehicles of three Panzer Divisions, the Trieste Motorised Division and Ariete Armoured Division outflanked Bir Hakheim by moving deep into the desert. They were hidden by a sandstorm, and by dawn were in position. The British had positioned their tanks behind the Gazala Line to operate as a swift counter-attacking force, but the 15th Panzer Division fell on the southernmost of these units, the 3rd Royal Tank Regiment and the 8th Hussars, devastating them. The British counter-attacked against the 21st Panzers, but with little effect. Meanwhile, the Italian Ariete Division overwhelmed the 3rd Indian Motorised

The 'Brescia' Division attacking the Gazala Line, by Steve Noon © Osprey Publishing Ltd. Taken from Warrior 169: Italian Soldier in North Africa 1941–43.

Brigade, but not until the Indians had knocked out over 50 tanks.

The Free French at Bir Hakheim were now totally surrounded. Koenig had 4,000 troops in his force, comprising of a half-brigade of Foreign Legion fighters (which included several anti-Nazi Germans) two battalions of colonial troops and marine infantry. They defended a box outpost with its own artillery and anti-aircraft support, surrounded by minefields and barbed wire.

The tanks of the Ariete Division fell on the defenders, whom Rommel expected to quickly collapse, but the French fought wave after wave of attackers with ferocity. The Italian tanks were wiped out. The Free French held out bravely against overwhelming odds for almost two weeks, when they ran out of ammunition. A British attempt to relieve the defenders had floundered, and although the French were supported by the RAF, dropping supplies and seeing off German aircraft, it was not enough. On the night of 8 June, Koenig led his remaining men through the encircling Axis forces to safety.

The brave resistance of the Free French had scuppered Rommel's plan for a swift and deadly outflanking attack. While Koenig's defenders fought, Rommel had been steadily forcing the British and Indian forces to the north to withdraw, in a chaotic battle that the British named the 'Cauldron', but enemy counter-attacks and artillery fire slowed him down, and he faced the usual problems of fuel and ammunition shortages. His army was caught between the troops defending the Gazala Line and the British tanks in reserve, but the British failed to seize the advantage, failing to concentrate their armour to impact on Rommel's advance. Unchallenged, Rommel ordered a massive assault on the defensive position held by the Yorkshire battalions of the 150th Brigade, in order to secure a passage westwards through which supplies were beginning to trickle through to the German forces. Despite an admirable defence, the Yorkshiremen were overwhelmed, yet still the British commanders failed to decisively counter-attack with their tanks.

Just after the fall of Bir Hakheim, on 11 June, Rommel's three German divisions destroyed the remaining positions on the Gazala Line, and moved north to seize the Via Balbia. The South Africans and 50th Division near the coast were ordered to withdraw to the Egyptian border to avoid the same fate – the hurried retreat that ensued became known as the 'Gazala Gallop'. This left Tobruk exposed. The Italian infantry encircled it from the east, while Rommel moved his German divisions from the south to complete the siege, although under punishing firepower from RAF Hurricanes and P-40 Kittyhawk fighter-bombers.

From 15–17 June, the British mounted Operation *Battleaxe* to clear Axis forces from eastern Cyrenaica and raise the siege of Tobruk. However, the British lost over half of their tanks on the first day and on the second day, despite standing firm against a large German counter-attack against their centre, their western flank was pushed back. The Germans attempted to encircle the attackers on the third day of the operation, and the British only just managed to extricate their remaining forces in time to avoid disaster. Tobruk remained under siege.

Autoblinda Lince scout car

THE FALL OF TOBRUK

Tobruk was now mainly defended by the inexperienced 2nd South African Division, commanded by Major General Hendrik Klopper. Many of its defences had been re-used to protect the Gazala Line, and the Royal Navy, hampered by an influx of U-boats drawn from the Atlantic to the Mediterranean, did not have sufficient ships to adequately supply the port by sea. At dawn on 20 June, the entire German air force stationed in the Mediterranean, along with the Italian air force – the *Regia Aeronautica* – ravaged Tobruk in combination with a devastating artillery bombardment, while German pioneer battalions cleared a route through the minefields. The attackers advanced through the town, capturing the port in a single day. Four thousand tons of oil, and a hoard of provisions, vehicles and weapons fell to the Axis. Hitler immediately promoted Rommel to the esteemed rank of *Generalfeldmarschall*, and was now sure that this marked the beginning of the end for the British Empire. Indeed, rumours of the imminent arrival of the Germans sparked panic in Cairo, whose European inhabitants prepared to evacuate.

The 15th and 21st Panzer Divisions, with the 90th Light Division, now pursued the fleeing 8th Army. The 10th Indian Division was caught at Mersa Matruh, with 7,000 men captured, while the New Zealand Division to the south had to make a desperate night attack to break through the 21st Panzer Division.

A British reconnaissance force on patrol

THE FIRST BATTLE OF EL ALAMEIN

Auchinleck took personal command over the British forces, and chose a small railway stop by the sea called El Alamein as the location of his stand. To the south of this position lay impassable marshland, almost impossible for Rommel to use in an outflanking manoeuvre. But the morale of the British was rock bottom and desertions surged. The only advantage for the British lay with Ultra, which provided them with detailed information of Rommel's plans. Rommel's impatience to finish the 8th Army also proved beneficial to the British. When on 1 July he attacked the defences at El Alamein with the 90th Light Division, he failed to perform any reconnaissance and the attackers were driven back by heavy artillery fire. The 21st Panzer Division stormed a position held by the 18th Indian Brigade, but lost a third of its tanks, mostly to RAF fighter-bombers. Auchinleck ordered swift hit-and-run counter-attacks, and concentrated his artillery fire to great effect. The New Zealand Division pushed back the Ariete Division in a lightning attack that caught the Italians by surprise. On 3 July,

Rommel was forced to go on the defensive, with fewer than 50 serviceable tanks and his troops low on ammunition and fuel, and utterly exhausted.

The 8th Army used this reprieve to consolidate its defensive positions. It was too badly weakened to counter-attack, despite the arrival of Australian reinforcements. Rommel attacked again on 10 July, but the Italians near El Alamein were repulsed by the 9th Australian Division supported by a brigade of tanks. Throughout July, the two sides kept attacking and counter-attacking, but the Germans had the worst of it, as the RAF and the Royal Navy were again gaining dominance over the Mediterranean, causing great damage to Axis ports and convoys. Rommel's own air support suffered a devastating blow when, on the night of 26 July, the newly formed SAS (Special Air Service) in jeeps destroyed almost 40 aircraft at the German airfield near Fuka.

A Vickers light tank of the 7th Armoured Divison supports Commonwealth infantry

British carrier section

ENTER MONTGOMERY

Auchinleck's cautious defensive tactics had halted Rommel's advance into Egypt, but Churchill wanted a more aggressive commander-in-chief, so replaced him with General Harold Alexander. He also promoted Lieutenant General Gott, commander of XIII Corps, to command the 8th Army. But Gott was killed when his plane was shot down, and Lieutenant General Bernard Montgomery took his place.

Throughout August, the two sides faced each other, Montgomery building up the strength of the 8th Army, while Rommel faced shortages of fuel and reinforcements as Axis convoys succumbed to the RAF and Royal Navy in the Mediterranean. On 30 August, persuaded that supplies were imminent, and would be rushed to the front, Rommel attacked the British line in the south, hoping to break through and savage the 8th Army from the rear. Montgomery was well-prepared. Forewarned by Ultra, his tanks were ready to pounce on the attacking German armour. He had also extended the minefields that protected the southern end of the line, and these forced Rommel's panzers to advance along a narrow corridor, which proved an easy killing ground for the Desert Air Force's bombers and fighter-bombers. It took Rommel's forces an entire harrowing night to negotiate the minefields, and he was forced to continue the attack in the light of day. His goal was the Alam Halfa Ridge, but it was too well defended for the panzers to break through – a preliminary aerial bombardment had been thwarted as British fighter squadrons scattered the attacking Stukas. Rommel halted, hoping to draw out the defenders and envelop their counter-attack, but the counter-attack did not come – Montgomery held firm. To make things worse, Ultra had picked up the position of the convoy bringing Rommel's promised fuel and the British fleet and air force had annihilated it. With insufficient fuel, Rommel had no choice but to withdraw, leaving the Alamein Line intact. Apart from a desultory counter-attack by XXX Corps in the south, the British allowed the enemy to retreat.

Again, the enemies faced off against each other. The Axis troops suffered rampant illness, and a lack of all basic supplies. In October, overcome by stress, Rommel returned to Germany on sick leave. *General der Panzertruppe* Georg Stumme, commanded in Rommel's absence. He laid down half a million mines in front of the Afrika Korps' positions, convinced that Montgomery would soon go on the offensive. Instead, Montgomery was reinforcing his position slowly, unwilling to launch an attack until he was sure that he had overwhelming superiority and that his new reinforcements were adequately trained. By late October, with 8th Army's strength increased to a thousand tanks, bolstered by the inclusion of the newly arrived American Sherman tanks. Montgomery was ready.

THE SECOND BATTLE OF EL ALAMEIN

Operation *Lightfoot* involved an attack on the Axis' most heavily defended sector in the north. To misdirect the Germans, Montgomery employed a ruse devised by Major Jasper Maskelyne, a professional stage magician in civilian life. Hundreds of dummy vehicles and a fake water pipe line were installed in the south, while the illusion of a massive mobilisation was generated by trucks driving around with chains kicking up dust and radios broadcasting misleading orders.

The Axis airfields were severely disrupted on 19 October by raids from the Desert Air Force and squadrons of the US Middle East Army Air Force, the first American units to assemble on North African soil. On the evening of 23 October, Montgomery's artillery unleashed hell on the Axis positions, while Allied bombers ravaged the reserve and rear positions. Stumme did not have the shells spare to respond with his own guns. After dark, Allied sappers created corridors through the minefields, marking out safe areas with white tape and oil lamps. At 2200, XXX Corps advanced along these corridors with the 51st Highlanders (bagpipes skirling), 9th Australian, 1st South African and 2nd New Zealand divisions, each supported by at least one armoured regiment. However, the tanks of the X Corps became disorganised in the minefields, causing confusion and delay.

Montgomery's intricate deception to the south had failed to divert German units to reinforce the southern part of the line, despite a feint attack by the XIII Corps. Axis resistance was much stronger than expected, and threatened to stall the advance. But the Germans suffered an unexpected calamity when General Stumme, driven to the front to view the situation, was abandoned by his driver when his vehicle came under fire, and collapsed dead with heart failure. General von Thoma took over command, and was joined on 25 October by Rommel, who returned from Germany following news of Montgomery's offensive.

The British advance renewed with fresh vigour following the capture of German maps detailing the minefields by the Australians, who then proceeded to seize a vital hill during a night attack, and held out against heavy counter-attacks the following day. The tanks of XXX Corps and X Corps were beginning to mass beyond the minefields at this point, and Rommel reinforced the northern part of the line with the 21st Panzer Division. But over half his panzers had by now been destroyed, and the remnants did not have the fuel necessary to wage the kind of highly mobile war that Rommel excelled at. Regardless, Montgomery was forced to replace his original plan with a new offensive, Operation *Supercharge*, assaulting dug-in anti-tank guns with the 9th Armoured Brigade. Despite preliminary air attacks and an artillery bombardment, the brigade was utterly destroyed. The New Zealanders advanced far to the north, but German counter-attacks prevented a decisive breakthrough.

Rommel eventually started to plan a general withdrawal. His force was doomed without fuel and reinforcements. Montgomery was waging a battle of attrition that the Germans could not win. Hitler was furious, and commanded Rommel to stand and repulse the British, or die in the attempt. Rommel was incredulous, but nevertheless obeyed. As he expected, the British broke through and captured the Afrika Korps headquarters, seizing General Thoma prisoner. Unwilling to sacrifice any more of his force to Hitler's demands, Rommel issued the order to withdraw once more, and his force retreated all the way across Libya. The Italian infantry were left far behind by the mobile German forces, and thousands were captured by the advancing British. Montgomery did not rush ahead, but pushed forward carefully, unwilling to risk losing his advantage as had so often happened to the British in North Africa under previous commanders. He was well aware that his army had to be well supplied to follow the Germans across the deserts of Libya, and that his troops had to be in excellent fighting shape if they were to continue the fight into German-held territory.

Thanks to the slow pace of Montgomery's pursuit, Rommel managed to extricate most of his force to safety, but the British had struck the first significant blow against the might of the German war machine in North Africa. However, it would fall to the Americans, soon to land their forces on the coast of Algeria, to help deal the killing strike.

British armour rumbles past a desert town

FIGHTING THE DUEL IN THE DESERT USING *BOLT ACTION*

Rommel's relentless advance through the desert and his abrupt change of fortune following the stubborn British resistance at El Alamein are arguably the iconic actions of the North African desert campaign, and make ideal material for thrilling games of *Bolt Action*.

THEATRE SELECTORS

The following theatre selectors should be used to represent the forces involved in the Duel in the Desert:

GERMANS
- Up to and including the Second Battle of El Alamein: Rommel Triumphant Reinforced Platoon (*Armies of Germany*, page 77).
- After the Second Battle of El Alamein: Rommel's Defeat Reinforced Platoon (*Armies of Germany*, page 79).

ITALIANS
- War in Africa Reinforced Platoon (*Armies of Italy and the Axis*, page 31).

BRITISH & COMMONWEALTH
- Operation *Compass* Reinforced Platoon (*Armies of Great Britain*, page 72) – represents the state of the British army in North Africa up until Montgomery took command of the 8th Army.
- Operation *Lightfoot* Reinforced Platoon (*Armies of Great Britain*, page 74) – represents Montgomery's re-equipped and reformed 8th Army.
- Any Indian-based force can use the Indian Division Reinforced Platoon (page 23).
- Behind Enemy Lines Reinforced Platoon (*Armies of Great Britain*, page 73) – for battles fought after July 1942, you can choose SAS Infantry Squads (see page 59).

FREE FRENCH
- Free French Reinforced Platoon (page XX) – representing the defenders of Bir Hakheim (see page 19).

Panzer II

DUEL IN THE DESERT SPECIAL RULES

The following special rules are pertinent to battles fought in this campaign:

MULTINATIONAL FORCES
The Afrika Korps fought beside the Italian army in countless engagements throughout Rommel's North African campaign. Refer to the rules on page 120 if you want to field multinational forces.

DESERT WARFARE
These battles were fought in the Egyptian and Libyan deserts. See the rules for Desert Warfare, on page 121.

DESERT FIGHTERS
Before the First Battle of El Alamein, the British 8th Army has seen plenty of action in the desert, so any Veteran units in any British and Commonwealth forces have the Desert Fighters special rule (page 122) for free. All units in a Behind Enemy Lines Reinforced Platoon have the Desert Fighters rule for free, as they specialise in fighting in this terrain.

Regular British and Commonwealth units may or may not have had enough training or experience of desert warfare, as some of these would be replacement units recently arrived at the front, so you have to purchase the Desert Fighters special rule for them at +2pts per man. Inexperienced units definitely have had no experience of this style of fighting, so can't be given this rule.

Up to the First Battle of El Alamein, German Veteran or Regular units can be bought the Desert Fighters special rule (+2pts per man) representing any preliminary training they have had. The same goes for Italian Veteran and Regular units – they are better organised under the command of the Germans and so are able to put their extensive experience of desert fighting to better use than at the start of the North African conflict.

From the First Battle of El Alamein onwards, all Regular and Veteran German, Italian, British and Commonwealth units in North Africa have the Desert Fighters rule for free – by now they've learnt the hard way how to fight in the desert.

All units in a Free French force have the Desert Fighter special rule for free – they've been trained to fight in this environment since before the war.

ROMMEL'S GENIUS

Rommel was a master at utilising his tanks to great effect in the vast expanse of the desert. He would drive his armoured formations at great speed through the wilderness, widely dispersing them in small groups of mixed arms. Then, when a target was pinpointed, he would concentrate his forces in a well-coordinated attack, sweeping his armour from the desert against enemy positions in a swift outflanking manoeuvre.

To represent this, an Axis player fighting a battle between the arrival of the Afrika Korps and up to (but not including) the First Battle of El Alamein can use the following rule:

When the Axis player is about to move an outflanking unit onto the table, if that unit is motorised (i.e. a vehicle, towed artillery or infantry in a transport), he can choose whether it does so on the left or right table edge – no need for any written instructions!

COMMAND FROM THE FRONT

Rommel commanded in person from the front in his Storch airplane. This ensured that he was informed of exactly what was happening in the forward positions, and so could implement clear orders at once to his troops.

To represent this, an Axis player fighting a battle between the arrival of the Afrika Korps and up to (but not including) the First Battle of El Alamein can use the following rules. German and Italian Air Observers can radio in Rommel's Storch by simply being ordered to *fire* (but that turn they cannot shoot, nor call in an air strike). Roll a die at the beginning of the following turn. On a 1 nothing happens and you can roll again next turn. On a 2+, the player's force counts as being under the direct control of Rommel himself – all Axis officers increase their Morale Bonus by +1, and Axis reserves do not suffer the –1 penalty to their morale check for moving onto the table.

THE ALLIED RETREAT

Up until the First Battle of El Alamein, the Allies are retreating in confusion and disorder from Rommel's push. To represent this, for any games set before the encounters at El Alamein, Allied players cannot use outflanking manoeuvres, except where noted.

Vickers light tank Mk C

NIGHT FIGHTING

Much raiding between the opposing sides took place at night, and fighting at night was an integral part of Montgomery's tactics during *Operation* Lightfoot. Indeed, for any engagement fought as part of Operation *Lightfoot*, the British player can choose whether to fight at night or not, unless he is for some reason the defender.

Afrika Korps kradschützen

For the full rules on night fighting, see page 129.

MINEFIELDS

Minefields were used extensively throughout this period of the war in North Africa – see page 131 for the full rules on minefields. In fact, minefields were so ubiquitous in desert warfare that we recommend that you use these rules as a matter of course, if you want to play a more historically accurate game.

CONTROL OF THE SKIES

Command of the air swung back and forth at this stage of the North African campaign – see page 125. The Axis has control of the skies between the arrival of the Afrika Korps and the First Battle of El Alamein. From the battles at El Alamein onwards, the Allies enjoy control of the skies – being joined by one of the first units of the US Army Air Force to fight in the war, and now outnumbering the beleaguered *Luftwaffe* and *Regia Aeronautica* in North Africa.

TANK BATTLES

Rommel was an expert in using his tank formations to charge across the desert and outflank the hapless Allied forces. If you are the proud owner of the *Tank War* supplement for *Bolt Action*, and have enough tanks at your disposal, it would be churlish not to replay some of the great desert encounters between the panzers of the Afrika Korps and the tanks of the British army. A desert wargames table, uncluttered with obstacles, is ideal for the dashing sweep of tabletop tank warfare.

The *Tank War* book allows players to create opposing Armoured Platoons, and you can use the Tank Battle scenario on page 20 of that supplement to represent a generic clash of armour in the North African desert.

On page 53, the Operation *Supercharge* scenario allows you to fight one of the definitive actions of the Second Battle of El Alamein as a tank battle, as is right and proper.

Note that you can either use the scenario's Dust Storm special rule, or implement the more detailed rules for Desert Warfare found in this book, on page 121.

LIMITED FUEL SUPPLY

To represent the problems of supplying the armies stretched across the vast distances of the North African deserts, use the rules on limited fuel supply – see page 133. The Allies should be affected by this rule for battles fought between the arrival of the Afrika Korps and the First Battle of El Alamein. Rommel utilized his planes to destroy British petrol lorries wherever they could be found, and to disrupt British supply lines. At the First Battle of El Alamein and for subsequent battles, the Afrika Korps should be affected by a limited fuel supply, as the Royal Navy and RAF eroded the Axis supply lines across the Mediterranean.

USING CAPTURED ENEMY VEHICLES

The rules for using captured enemy vehicles are particularly pertinent for this stage of the fighting in North Africa – see page 133.

SCENARIOS

GENERAL SCENARIOS

For actions fought before the First Battle of El Alamein, when Rommel's Afrika Korps was pushing back the British forces, the following scenarios from the *Bolt Action* rulebook are suitable, with the Axis as attackers:

- Scenario 1: Envelopment (page 108)
- Scenario 2: Maximum Attrition (page 110)
- Scenario 3: Point Defence (page 112)
- Scenario 4: Hold Until Relieved (page 114)

Note that a Behind Enemy Lines Reinforced Platoon will be actively taking the fight to the enemy, in an attempt to slow the German advance, so any battle involving the LRDG can feature them as the attackers instead. Ideal scenarios to represent their exploits would be:

- Scenario 2: Maximum Attrition (page 110)
- Scenario 5: Top Secret (page 115)
- Scenario 6: Demolition (page 116)

Games that represent Allied counter-attacks, such as Operation *Battleaxe* to relieve Tobruk, should have the Allies as attackers, using any scenario from the *Bolt Action* rulebook.

The Free French resistance at Bir Hakheim can be played out as a Hold Until Relieved scenario.

We've included three special scenarios to represent battles fought by the British against the Afrika Korps: Skirmish in the Sand (page 51), The Siege of Tobruk (page 52) and Lightfoot (page 56). The latter two scenarios are based on actions that might have occurred during those two seminal battles. The first one is a more generic scenario that re-enacts a typical encounter in the desert between two opposing patrols.

After the Second Battle of El Alamein, the Axis side is now in retreat. The first four scenarios in the *Bolt Action* rulebook can be used to represent actions fought during Rommel's withdrawal, but with the British as the attackers.

TERRAIN

Refer to the section on desert terrain on page 121 for advice on how to set up a North African battlefield.

Humber armoured cars lead a British recce probe

SCENARIO 5: SKIRMISH IN THE SAND

"Before his relief arrived, Stone decided to take his tank and the other on outpost duty with him. They motored a little way south before creeping up the gently sloping ridge in front of them, using for cover a shallow valley or re-entrant that ran up towards the crest of the ridge at right angles. As they neared their objective, expecting the crack of an enemy shot at any moment, the tanks slowed to a crawl to keep their noise and dust down. Then, suddenly, 'not two hundred yards away was a 50mm anti-tank gun pointing straight at me, and fifteen yards away from it were the crew, frolicking over their breakfast in their slit trenches.' Stone looked to the left of this little party of Germans, spotting a couple of machine-gun nests. Then turning to the right of the gun, further along the ridge, he saw something else – perhaps some piece of artillery equipment. Stone was amazed that he had made it so close without being detected. These anti-tank guns had driven him mad at times during the proceeding weeks, but now he had the opportunity for revenge…" – *The Tank War,* Mark Urban

The following scenario allows you to recreate one of the many confusing skirmishes that took place in the North African desert, where a patrol has a sudden, unexpected close encounter with the enemy. Fighting in the desert could be a disorientating experience, and despite the apparent bleakness of the environment, hidden gullies, low ridges or the subtle undulation of sand hills could hide enemy units from each other until they were almost nose-to-nose.

FORCES

This scenario is designed to be played with equal points values on both sides. Any of the reinforced platoons mentioned on page 48 can represent the forces involved. One player must be the attacker, the other the defender.

This scenario works best with a small *Bolt Action* force, so players should be restricted to no more than 500pts each.

If both players agree, for an unusual game (perhaps re-enacting the tank versus artillery/machine-gunner episode related above, for example), both sides can ignore the usual restrictions on selecting units. Be warned, though, that this might result in an unbalanced game – one solution is for both players to sit down together and create each force jointly, so as to design an interesting and more balanced encounter.

SET-UP

TERRAIN

The scenario takes place somewhere in the Libyan or Egyptian desert (see Desert Warfare, page 121). However, terrain is not

set up before the battle as usual. It's put down as part of the deployment phase, as explained next.

DEPLOYMENT

Each player will need a small scrap of identical paper for each unit, and must briefly but clearly write down on one side the unit's name or description. Each scrap needs to be folded over to conceal the writing. An identical number of blank scraps, likewise folded over, are also required.

All scraps from both sides, plus the blanks, are then placed in a cup, bag or other container and mixed up.

Then divide the table into a number of sections of equal dimensions. The number of sections is equal the length of your table in feet. So for example, a 6' x 4' table must be divided into six equal-sized sections (six 2' x 2' sections).

Starting with the defender, each player now takes it in turn to place a piece of desert terrain on the table – the terrain must be placed at least 6" from another terrain piece already placed. When a player places a terrain piece, he must also draw a scrap from the container and place it still folded (no peeking!) anywhere on top of or adjacent to that terrain.

Continue placing terrain (and scraps) until you either run out of terrain or scraps. Alternatively, a player can announce that he is passing as long as each section of the table has got terrain in it (even partially). The opposing player can then, if he wishes, place one more terrain piece (and scrap) before moving onto the next step.

After terrain placement, all scraps remaining in the container are discarded without looking at them.

Then, starting with the defender, each player takes it in turn to reveal one scrap of paper. It's unfolded, and the associated unit, if any, is placed by its controller in or adjacent to the terrain piece.

After all scraps on the table have been revealed, each player rolls a D6, re-rolling ties. The player who scores highest chooses one long table edge as his edge. His opponent has the opposite side as his edge.

The set-up phase then ends. All units that have not been placed on the table are in reserve.

SPECIAL RULES

FIRST TURN
The battle begins.

DESERT WARFARE
Use the rules for Desert Warfare for this scenario (see page 121).

OBJECTIVE

Both sides must attempt to destroy the other whilst preserving their own forces.

GAME DURATION

Keep a count of how many turns have elapsed as the game is played. At the end of turn 6, roll a die. On a result of 1, 2 or 3 the game ends, on a roll of 4, 5 or 6 play one further turn.

VICTORY!

At the end of the game, calculate which side has won by adding up victory points as follows. If one side scores at least 2 more victory points than the other then that side has won a

clear victory. Otherwise the result is deemed too close to call and honours are shared – a draw!

Players score 1 victory point for every enemy unit destroyed.

8th Army light mortar team

SCENARIO 6: THE SIEGE OF TOBRUK

Tobruk was the one rock that stood firm against Rommel's inexorable advance. Churchill urged that the port should be held "to the death without thought of retirement." From the 10 April to 27 November 1941, the forces defending Tobruk stood firm against Rommel's surrounding troops. The siege was lifted during the course of Operation *Crusader*. It remained in Allied hands until the defeat of the 8th Army at the Battle of Gazala in June 1942.

General Morshead, commander of the mainly Australian garrison until their replacement by Polish and British units in the autumn of 1941, declared that "there will be no Dunkirk here. If we should have to get out, we'll fight our way out. There is to be no surrender and no retreat."

The following scenario allows you to recreate an action from one of Rommel's assaults on Tobruk during the early stages of the siege. The Axis troops are attempting to destroy one of the many perimeter posts surrounding the port, and create a breach to penetrate further into the Allied defences. Note that you can adapt this scenario for use in any World War II theatre where one side is attempting to destroy the other's defensive position.

THE RATS OF TOBRUK

The defenders of Tobruk were the first soldiers to stop the German forces in the North African campaign. Lord Haw-Haw, during his notorious radio broadcasts, contemptuously referred to them as "poor desert rats of Tobruk." The 9th Australian Division who garrisoned the port proudly adopted this nickname and even designed their own rat-shaped medals, crafted from scrap metal taken from a German bomber

that they had downed with a captured German gun.

During the initial stages of the siege of Tobruk, the Rats concentrated on reinforcing their defences, and true to their name, constructed a warren of tunnels down which they could hide during air raids or artillery bombardment. As the siege progressed, the Rats began to take the fight to the besieging Germans, creeping out to capture an enemy soldier for interrogation, or making audacious night attacks to cause as much damage and panic as possible without getting caught.

A Rat patrol would crawl for several miles to reach an enemy position, quietly surround it, then rush it with bayonets, often capturing their objective without a shot being fired.

After an epic nine months under siege, the Rats were finally all withdrawn from Tobruk by October 1941, many reluctant to leave the job unfinished. This was a political decision, pushed by the Australian government which was keen to have all Australians in the Middle East fight under a unified command, as well as the concerns of Australians back home that the division had suffered too long without reinforcement.

During their stay at Tobruk, the Australians had suffered 3,000 casualties, with over 900 men taken prisoner. Their stubborn resistance was proof that the German army was not all-conquering at a time when Hitler's forces otherwise dominated every other arena of war.

FORCES

This scenario is designed to be played with equal points values on both sides.

It's a very good idea to use the rules on multinational forces (page 120) for the Axis in this game.

Commonwealth troops occupy the ruins of a shattered town.

The Allied defenders have to choose to field an anti-tank gun, a machine-gun and either an anti-tank team or a mortar team. These are vital to the defence of the perimeter post and so are mandatory choices from their theatre selector.

The defenders are determined to hold Tobruk at all costs, and to represent this, the British player can take an extra National Characteristic for free. He cannot choose any Inexperienced units.

The following reinforced platoons should be used to represent the forces involved:

GERMANS

- Rommel Triumphant Reinforced Platoon (*Armies of Germany*, page 77).

8th Army medium mortar team

ITALIANS

- War in Africa Reinforced Platoon (*Armies of Italy and the Axis*, page 31).

BRITISH & COMMONWEALTH

- Operation *Compass* Reinforced Platoon (*Armies of Great Britain*, page 72) – representing the 18th Australian Infantry Brigade.
- Indian Division Reinforced Platoon (page 23) – representing the dismounted 18th King Edward's Own Cavalry of the British Indian Army.

SET-UP

TERRAIN

Set up the terrain as shown on the scenario map. You'll need terrain to represent the frontal wire, minefield, anti-tank gun and machine-gun emplacements and trench systems. The rest of the table represents desert, but is clear of any other terrain.

DEPLOYMENT

The Allied player is the defender in this scenario, and sets up all of his units on his side of the table between the booby-trapped trench on his side up to the table middle line. These units can use the hidden set-up rules (see Hidden Set-up on page 117 of the *Bolt Action* rulebook). He must set up his anti-tank gun, machine-gun team and either an anti-tank team or a mortar team in the emplacements, so each emplacement is occupied.

The attacking Axis units are not set up on the table at the start of the game. The attacker must nominate at least half of his force to form his first wave. This can be his entire army if he wishes. Any units not included in the first wave are left in reserve.

Italian Carro Veloce
CV33

SPECIAL RULES

FIRST TURN

The battle begins. During Turn 1, the attacking player must move his entire first wave onto the table. These units can enter the table from any point on the attacker's table edge, and must be given either a *run* or *advance* order. Note that no order test is required to move units onto the table as part of the first wave.

FRONTAL WIRE

The barbed wire counts as an obstacle.

MINEFIELD

The minefield is littered with anti-tank mines and anti-personnel mines, and counts as a mixed minefield. See page 131 for the rules on minefields.

BOOBY-TRAPPED TRENCH

The trench counts as rough ground. In addition, the trench counts as an anti-personnel minefield. Infantry within the trench can use it as cover.

CRAWL TRENCH

This shallow trench counts as open ground, but infantry inside it count as being Dug-in (see page 124).

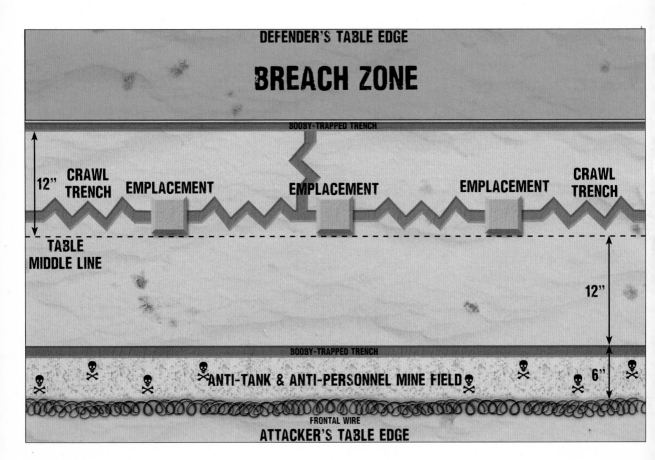

EMPLACEMENT

The emplacement allows the unit within it to be Dug-in (see page XX). Units deployed within an emplacement at the start of the game cannot move out of the emplacement (so cannot be given *advance* or *run* orders). They are dedicated to fight or die. They do not have to check morale as the result of losing men from shooting.

Afrika Korps medium mortar team

An emplacement is destroyed as soon as the unit occupying it is destroyed. Use a marker to show that an emplacement has been destroyed. A destroyed emplacement counts as a crawl trench and rough ground for the rest of the battle.

RESERVES – ATTACKER

The attacker cannot use outflanking manoeuvres during this scenario. The flanks of the perimeter post are well-defended by other Allied troops and well protected by mines.

DESERT WARFARE

Use the rules for Desert Warfare for this scenario (see page 121).

DESERT FIGHTERS

All Allied Veteran units have the Desert Fighters special rule (page 122) for free.

Any Axis Veteran or Regular units can be bought the Desert Fighters special rule (+2pts per man).

COMMAND FROM THE FRONT

Rommel isn't going to risk flying in his Storch plane near Tobruk's anti-aircraft guns, so the Axis player cannot use the Command From the Front rule in this game.

NIGHT FIGHTING

Rommel timed his assaults to take place at night, dawn or dusk, so this scenario uses the rules for night fighting (page 129).

CONTROL OF THE SKIES

The Axis has control of the skies around Tobruk, but the port is bristling with anti-aircraft guns, which offset this, so the Axis player does not gain any advantage during this scenario.

LIMITED FUEL SUPPLY

Tobruk is supplied from the sea by the Royal Navy, and Rommel has captured Allied supply dumps in his advance through Cyrenaica, so neither side has any problems with limited fuel supply during this scenario.

OBJECTIVE

The attacker must destroy all three emplacements (see special rules).

In addition, the attacker must try to move as many of units as he can into the Breach Zone (see map) or off the defender's table edge. The defender must try to stop him. Note that in this scenario, attacking units are allowed to deliberately move off the table from the defender's table edge to reach their objective.

GAME DURATION

Keep a count of how many turns have elapsed as the game is played. At the end of Turn 6, roll a die. On a result of 1, 2 or 3 the game ends, on a roll of 4, 5 or 6 play one further turn.

VICTORY!

At the end of the game, calculate which side has won by adding up victory points as follows. If one side scores at least 2 more victory points than the other then that side has won a clear victory. Otherwise the result is deemed too close to call and honours are shared – a draw!

The attacking player scores 1 victory point for every enemy unit destroyed.

In addition, if all three emplacements are destroyed, he also scores 2 victory points for each of his own units that is inside the Breach zone (even if only partially), and 3 victory points for each of his own units that has moved off the enemy table edge before the end of the game.

The British player scores 2 victory points for every enemy unit destroyed.

8th Army 25-pdr field gun

SCENARIO 7: OPERATION *LIGHTFOOT*

Operation *Lightfoot*, the preliminary phase of the Second Battle of El Alamein, was given this codename because Montgomery's plan involved the infantry attacking first in order to clear the extensive enemy minefields of the forward section posts planted among them. These advanced positions consisted of Axis infantry supported by a few anti-tank guns and machine-gun nests.

The advancing Allied infantry were too light to trip the anti-tanks mines, and when they had mopped up all resistance, engineers would move in behind them and carefully clear a lane through the minefield wide enough for a line of tanks to move through. Across the line of attack, each group of engineers were expected to clear an 8km route during the first night of the operation, but enemy resistance proved strong, the minefields proved too deep, and this objective had been only partially achieved by sunrise.

The following scenario is designed to recreate the first stage of Operation *Lightfoot*, when an infantry force picks its way through the enemy minefield to allow the Allied engineers to start their vital work in relative safety.

FORCES

This scenario is designed to be played with equal points values on both sides. The following reinforced platoons should be used to represent the forces involved:

GERMANS
- Rommel Triumphant Reinforced Platoon (*Armies of Germany*, page 77).

ITALIANS
- War in Africa Reinforced Platoon (*Armies of Italy and the Axis*, page 31).

Note – for this scenario, the Axis side has to take at least three infantry sections, one anti-tank gun and one machine-gun team. It cannot choose any armoured vehicles.

BRITISH & COMMONWEALTH
- Operation *Lightfoot* Reinforced Platoon (*Armies of Great Britain*, page 74) – represents Montgomery's re-equipped and reformed 8th Army.

Note – for this scenario, the Allied side cannot choose any artillery or armoured vehicles.

SET-UP

TERRAIN

The scenario is set in the desert – see page 121. Note that almost the entire tabletop counts as an anti-tank minefield, but you don't need to place minefield terrain everywhere on the table to represent this – see below.

Platoon, advance! The 8th Army moves up in good order.

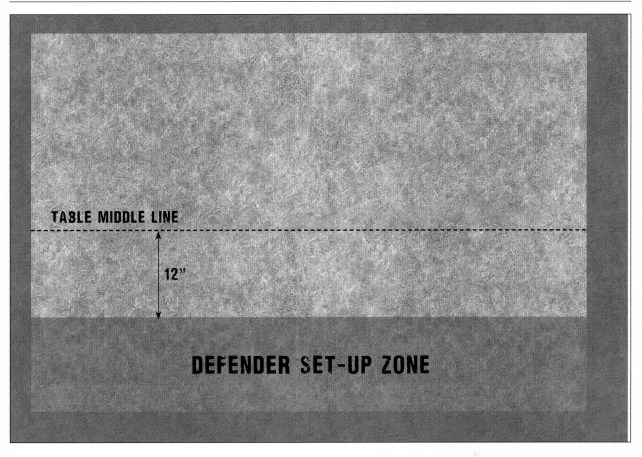

TABLE MIDDLE LINE

12"

DEFENDER SET-UP ZONE

DEPLOYMENT

In this scenario, the Axis side is defending.

The defender picks a side of the table and places three separate forward emplacements anywhere in his set-up zone (see map). Each emplacement is made of three linear obstacles up to 6" long and 1" tall, representing hard cover like sandbags, a section of low wall or earthwork, which are always placed as shown in the diagram at right. These are placed by the player so that they are at least 6" from the defender's table edge, and at least 18" from each other.

Note that an Italian force does not get any additional emplacements (effectively these being the D3 emplacements it normally gets when defending).

The defender now sets up his entire force within his set-up zone. At least one infantry unit must be deployed within each emplacement. An artillery unit must be placed within one of the emplacements.

The attacker's units are not set up on the table at the start of the game. The attacker must nominate at least half of his force to form his first wave. This can be his entire army if he wishes. Any units not included in the first wave are left in reserve.

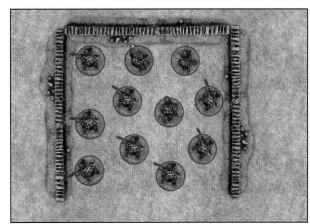

SPECIAL RULES

PREPARATORY BOMBARDMENT

Montgomery unleashed the largest concentration of artillery since World War I at the start of Operation *Lightfoot*. A Preparatory Bombardment automatically strikes the defender's positions (see page 118, *Bolt Action*). To represent the scale of the bombardment, when the first bombardment has been resolved, immediately resolve a second, but this time with a −1 on the dice rolls on the preparatory bombardment chart!

FIRST TURN
During Turn 1, the attacker must move his entire first wave onto the table. These units can enter the table from any point on the attacker's table edge, and must be given either a *run* or *advance* order. Note that no order test is required to move units onto the table as part of the first wave.

MULTINATIONAL FORCES
Rommel's forces can be a mix of German and Italian units. Refer to the rules on page 120 if you want to field multinational forces.

DESERT WARFARE
This scenario is set in the desert. See the rules for Desert Warfare, on page 121.

DESERT FIGHTERS
All units on the both sides have the Desert Fighters special rule (page 122) for free. By now, both sides are highly experienced desert fighters.

COMMAND FROM THE FRONT
Rommel is on leave in Germany during this stage of the battle, so obviously cannot influence events in this scenario.

NIGHT FIGHTING
This stage of Operation *Lightfoot* took place at night. For the full rules on night fighting, see page 129.

MINEFIELDS
Apart from the areas covered by the emplacements, the entire battlefield is one big anti-tank minefield – see page 131 for the full rules on minefields. The mines are mostly anti-tank mines, which cannot be tripped by infantry. However, there are patches of anti-personnel mines scattered about. The defender has three additional minefield sections per full 1,000 points of his force.

CONTROL OF THE SKIES
From the battles at El Alamein onwards, the Allies enjoy control of the skies – the RAF are joined by one of the first units of the US Army Air Force to fight in the war, and now outnumber the beleaguered *Luftwaffe* in North Africa. See page 125 for the rules on control of the skies.

LIMITED FUEL SUPPLY
Only a fraction of the fuel supplies promised by Rommel's Italian allies in North Africa and by his superiors in Germany have materialized, and his vehicles are now severely depleted of petrol – the Axis side is affected by the rules on limited fuel supply (see page 133).

RADIO JAMMING
During the opening stages of Operation *Lightfoot*, Wellington bombers equipped with special jamming equipment flew over the battlefields disrupting the enemy's radio communications, causing utter confusion. To represent this, on the first turn of the game, all Axis officers reduce their officer morale modifier by −1. At the end of each game turn, the Axis player rolls a D6. If he scores less than the current game turn number, the jamming stops and his officers' morale modifiers are returned to normal.

HIGHLANDER BAGPIPES
If the Allied player is fielding a force representing the Highlanders of 51st Division, who fought in Operation *Lightfoot*, and he has any models playing the bagpipes, he can add up to one piper per Highlander infantry section for free. The piper counts as a member of that unit, but cannot shoot (though he can fight in close quarters – imagine him smashing the pipes over an opponent's head). A unit with a piper can re-roll any morale check it has to make.

OBJECTIVE
The attacker must try to capture the three emplacements – the defender must try to stop him.

GAME DURATION
Keep a count of how many turns have elapsed as the game is played. At the end of Turn 6, roll a die. On a result of 1, 2 or 3 the game ends, on a roll of 4, 5 or 6 play one further turn.

VICTORY!
At the end of the game, calculate which side has won as follows: the attacking player wins if the defender does not hold any emplacements at the end of the game. The defender wins if he holds at least one emplacement at the end of the game – the area must be totally secured by the attackers, otherwise the arrival of the engineers will be delayed and Montgomery's plan will fall into disarray.

To hold an emplacement there must be a model from one of your infantry or artillery units touching or within the emplacement at the end of the turn, and there must be no enemy infantry or artillery models touching or within it.

An emplacement that has no models touching or within it is not held by any side.

ADDITIONAL UNITS
BRITAIN & THE COMMONWEALTH

SAS INFANTRY SQUAD

Founded in 1941 by David Stirling, a lieutenant in the Scots Guards and member of No.8 Commando, this force was formed to operate deep inside enemy-controlled territory, disrupting enemy supply chains, sabotaging airfields and gleaning valuable intelligence.

The SAS was initially based in North Africa, and its first mission, Operation *Squatter*, took place on 16 November 1941. In support of Operation *Crusader*, the force of five officers and 60 troopers was dropped by parachute at night behind enemy lines and tasked with attacking the airfields at Gazala and Timimi. Strong winds scattered the force, and enemy resistance was fiercer than expected. It was a disaster, with a third of the force killed or captured.

Stirling was given one more chance, and this time he showed what the SAS was capable of. With fresh recruits, the force was transported through the Libyan sands by the Long Range Desert Group to attack its three target airfields. Sixty enemy aircraft were destroyed, without the loss of a single man.

Subsequent missions, throughout 1942 to 1943, saw them creating chaos and destruction at enemy held harbours and airfields in Libya, Crete and Rhodes. On many missions, the SAS teamed up with the LRDG, who provided them with transport or sometimes joined in with the operations. In September 1942, the force was renamed the 1st SAS Regiment and consisted of four British squadrons, one Free French Squadron, one Greek Squadron, and the Special Boat Section (SBS).

In July 1943, the newly formed 2nd SAS participated in the Allied invasion of Sicily, with an amphibious attack to seize ground before the main invasion force arrived, and a parachute drop onto north Sicily to disrupt the enemy. Later that year, units of the SAS were parachuted into mainland Italy to rescue escaped prisoners of war, and other units raided by sea to destroy railroad bridges. Their operations in the Mediterranean ended when they were withdrawn to Great Britain to prepare for their role in the Normandy landings in 1944.

Cost: Veteran Infantry 72pts
Composition: 1 NCO and 3 men
Weapons: Pistol and rifle
Options:

- Add up to 4 additional men with pistol and rifle for +18pts each.
- Any man can replace his rifle with a submachine gun for +2pts.
- Up to two men may have a light machine gun for +20pts. For each LMG, another man becomes the loader.
- Light machine guns can be upgraded to Vickers K LMG for a further +5pts each.
- The squad can be given anti-tank grenades for +2pts per man.

Special Rules:

- Who Dares Wins! To represent their special training and motivation, units of SAS have the Fanatics special rule.
- Behind Enemy Lines: When Outflanking as described on page 119 of the *Bolt Action* rulebook, units of SAS ignore the −1 modifier to the Order test for coming onto the table.
- Tank Hunters (if antitank grenades taken).
- Vickers K Gun: The Vickers K gun (also known as the VGO) was a rapid firing machine gun developed for aircraft but also favoured by special forces. A Vickers K shoots with +1 dice compared to a regular LMG: 4 dice instead of 3.

SELECTORS

The SAS Infantry Squad is an Infantry Squad for the purposes of the generic Reinforced Platoon selector from the *Bolt Action* rulebook. It is also an Infantry Squad for the following theatre selectors of the *Armies of Great Britain* book: Raiders!, Behind Enemy Lines, Operation *Lightfoot*, Tunisia, Normandy, Into the Reich.

SAS section

LEGENDS OF BRITAIN & THE COMMONWEALTH

PADDY MAYNE

Robert Blair 'Paddy' Mayne (1915–55) was one of the most highly decorated soldiers in the British Army in World War II. A lawyer and an Irish rugby union international, he was one of the founding members of the SAS and led many daring raids against the Axis forces in North Africa and then in mainland Europe. He was responsible for destroying an unbelievable number of enemy aircraft and supply depots, as well as fighting in some brutal and decisive small unit actions. His fighting ability was only surpassed by his amazing charisma – many of the officers and men that fought alongside him stated that 'even in the darkest moments, Paddy's presence would make it feel like everything was going to be all right' – a great testament to his leadership skills.

Cost: 225pts (Veteran)

Team: 1 officer and up to 2 other men

Weapons: Submachine gun, pistol or rifle/carbine as depicted on the model

Options: Paddy may be accompanied by up to 2 men at a cost of +18pts per man

- The squad can be given anti-tank grenades for +2pts per man.

Special Rules: Who Dares Wins! To represent their special training and motivation, Paddy and his men have the Fanatics special rule.

- Behind Enemy Lines. When Outflanking as described on page 119 of the *Bolt Action* rulebook, Paddy and his men ignore the –1 modifier to the Order test for coming onto the table.
- Tank Hunters (if antitank grenades taken).
- Superb Leader: Paddy's Morale bonus is +4 and the range of his ability is 12".
- Special Mission: if Paddy is in your force, any SAS units left in Reserve can go on a special mission. These units must Outflank (even in scenarios that do not allow Outflanking) and, when they become available, they can enter the battlefield from either the declared short edge or any point along the enemy's table edge.

bush!

COMMAND ARMOURED TRUCKS (DORCHESTER, GUY LIZARD, ETC.)

The British-built small numbers of dedicated armoured command vehicles, based on truck chassis, like the AEC series and the Guy Lizard. The AEC 4x4 ACV was the most common armoured command vehicle of the British Army. It first saw service in North Africa in 1941, and was so big and comfortable inside that it soon became known as the 'Dorchester' after the luxury hotel in London. Two Dorchesters, captured by the Germans, were used by Rommel and his staff who affectionately named them as 'Max' and 'Moritz'. The Guy Lizard was an armoured command vehicle built by the British firm, Guy Motors. Most were lost during the retreat from France in 1940. Later, a few were utilised by the British 7th Armoured Division in North Africa.

Cost: 80pts (Inexperienced), 100pts (Regular), 120pts (Veteran)
Weapons: None
Damage Value: 7+ (armoured carrier)
Transport: Up to 10 men
Tow: Light howitzer; light or medium anti-tank gun; light anti-aircraft gun.
Special Rules:
• Command vehicle

SELECTORS
Command Armoured Trucks count as an Armoured Car for the purposes of the generic Reinforced Platoon selector from the *Bolt Action* rulebook. They also count as an Armoured Car for all of the theatre selectors of the *Armies of Great Britain* book (except for Raiders!, Behind Enemy Lines and Market Garden, where they cannot be used).

SCORPION FLAIL TANK
Developed in the summer of 1942, the "Matilda Scorpion" was a Matilda II tank fitted with a flail rotor at the front. The Matilda Scorpion was the most common mine-clearing tank in the African campaign. Twenty-five Matilda Scorpions, belonging to the 1st Army Tank Brigade's 42nd Royal Tank Regiment and 44th Royal Tank Regiments, took part in the Second Battle of El Alamein. A Mark II Scorpion was later developed by removing the turret. And when the first Grant tanks became available, they were also converted in this way to create the Mark III and IV Scorpions. The profile below can represent either a Matilda or a Grant-based tank.

Cost: 128pts (Inexperienced), 160pts (Regular), 192pts (Veteran)
Weapons: 1 turret-mounted light antitank gun with coaxial MMG
Damage Value: 9+ (medium tank)
Options:
• Remove the turret and weapons (making the Scorpion a Mark II) at a cost of −75pts
Special Rules:
• Slow
• Mine Flail: When you give this unit an *advance* order you can activate the mine flail. When the mine flail is active, it automatically clears any anti-personnel minefield sections the tank moves into. If it moves into an anti-tank minefield section, it clears it automatically, but the flail is destroyed and cannot be used any longer in the game. The model cannot fire in its front arc in the same turn it activates the mine flail.

SELECTORS
Scorpion tanks count as Tanks for the purposes of the generic Reinforced Platoon selector from the *Bolt Action* rulebook. They also count as Tanks for the following theatre selectors of the *Armies of Great Britain* book: Operation *Lightfoot*, Tunisia, Monte Cassino.

GERMANY

LORRAINE SCHLEPPER
The Lorraine 37L was a French tracked armoured vehicle originally designed to ferry fuel and ammunition to tank units on the battlefield. Following the fall of France in 1940, many of these were re-used by the Germans. Renamed the Lorraine Schlepper, the chassis of this vehicle fulfilled a number of roles in the German army: as the basis for a supply vehicle, a self-propelled anti-tank gun, and self-propelled artillery. About 40 chassis were converted to heavy field howitzers and sent to North Africa to support Rommel's mobile artillery. These slow and ungainly versions of the vehicle were attached to the 15th and 21st Panzer Divisions, and first used against the British at El Alamein in August 1942.

Cost: 92pts (Inexperienced), 115pts (Regular), 138pts (Veteran)
Weapons: 1 forward-facing medium anti-tank gun or medium howitzer
Damage Value: 7+ (armoured carrier)
Options:
• May exchange the main gun for either a heavy anti-tank gun or a heavy howitzer for +40pts
Special Rules:
• Open-topped

SELECTORS

The Lorraine Schlepper is a Tank Destroyer for the purposes of the generic Reinforced Platoon selector from the *Bolt Action* rulebook. It is also a Tank Destroyer for all theatre selectors of the *Armies of Germany* book that allow a Marder. It can be used in the following selectors relevant to the theatres described in this supplement: Rommel Triumphant Reinforced Platoon (*Armies of Germany*, page 77), Rommel's Defeat Reinforced Platoon (*Armies of Germany*, page 79), Defence of Italy Reinforced Platoon (*Armies of Germany*, page 85).

SD.KFZ 263 ARMOURED CAR

Based on the 232 series, the Sd.Kfz 263 *Panzerfunkwagen* was a dedicated command vehicle with a bedstead radio frame aerial. It saw extensive use in North Africa, where its speed made it a superb scouting vehicle for the type of long-range reconnaissance across the desert that Rommel required.

Cost: 84pts (Inexperienced), 105pts (Regular), 126pts (Veteran)
Weapons: 1 Hull-mounted forward facing MMG
Damage Value: 7+ (armoured car)
Special Rules:
- Recce (dual direction steering)
- Command Vehicle

SELECTORS

Sd.Kfz 263 command vehicles count as an Armoured Car for the purposes of the generic Reinforced Platoon selector from the *Bolt Action* rulebook. They also count as an Armoured Car for all of the theatre selectors of the *Armies of Germany* book (except for Operation *Mercury*, where they cannot be used).

SD.KFZ 6/3 "DIANA" HALFTRACK

The Sd.Kfz 6/3, or Diana, was a half-track vehicle reinforced with an armoured superstructure and fitted with a captured Soviet 76mm gun. A total of nine Sd.Kfz 6 transport halftracks were thus converted in early 1942 and were issued to the 605th *Panzerjaegerabteilung* in North Africa.

Cost: 96pts (Inexperienced), 120pts (Regular), 144pts (Veteran)
Weapons: 1 Hull-mounted forward facing medium anti-tank gun.
Damage Value: 7+ (armoured car)
Special Rules:
- Open-Topped

SELECTORS

Sd.Kfz 6/3 command vehicles count as a Tank Destroyer for the purposes of the generic Reinforced Platoon selector from the *Bolt Action* rulebook. They also count as a Tank Destroyer for the following selectors: Rommel Triumphant Reinforced Platoon (*Armies of Germany*, page 77), Rommel's Defeat Reinforced Platoon (*Armies of Germany*, page 79).

Afrika Korps PaK 38 anti-tank gun

THEATRE SELECTORS

RAMCKE BRIGADE

Originally formed to participate in the invasion of Malta, when that operation was cancelled, this brigade of elite German paratrooper units was sent to join Rommel's Afrika Korps in North Africa. Initially known as the *Fallschirmjäger-Brigade Afrika*, in April 1942 it was renamed the *Fallschirmjäger-Brigade Ramcke*, after its commander, Oberst Hermann-Bernhard Ramcke.

It proved particularly successful in countering the actions of the British Special Air Service, which had been causing such disruption behind the Axis lines.

During the German withdrawal after the Second Battle of El Alamein, the brigade became stranded behind enemy lines. Marching on foot through the desert to regroup with Rommel's forces, it managed to hijack a supply convoy of British transport vehicles, and when the brigade returned to its own lines, the food, water, cigarettes and fuel it brought with it was greatly appreciated.

It next saw action in Tunisia, where it was renamed *Luftwaffen-Jäger-Brigade 1*, due to Ramcke being transferred to Europe. Major Hans Kroh took over control.

The brigade continued to resist the Allies in the mountains of southern Tunisia until the surrender of the Afrika Korps in May 1943.

RAMCKE BRIGADE REINFORCED PLATOON

To field the Ramcke Brigade, use the *Fallschirmjäger* Reinforced Platoon on page 36, and include *General der Fallschirmtruppen* Hermann-Bernhard Ramcke.

Afrika Korps MMG team

LEGENDS OF GERMANY

GENERAL DER FALLSCHIRMTRUPPEN RAMCKE

Hermann-Bernhard Ramcke Hermann-Bernhard Ramcke was a pluri-decorated combat officer in World War I, but he remained in the *Wehrmacht* and at the beginning of World War II he applied for the newborn *Fallschirmjäger* corps and successfully qualified at the age of 51. He then fought as an officer in *Fallschirmjäger* units in pretty much all sectors of the European theatre, proving always a very capable and decisive leader, always showing great attention for the well-being of the men under his command and thus earning their respect. He took part in the assault on Crete and then fought in North Africa under Rommel. The most famous episode of this period was when he led his unit (named Ramcke Brigade) after the defeat at the second battle of El Alamein in a long retreat through the desert towards the Axis lines. Initially fighting off the pursuing British while retreating on foot, they captured a supply convoy and drove the rest of the way, returning to Rommel's command with a bounty of captured supplies.

Ramcke was evacuated back to Germany before the final collapse of the Afrika Korps, and then saw action again in the defence of Italy and then even on the Eastern front, where he was wounded. After a recovery stay in Germany, he was finally assigned to the defence of Brest on the Atlantic coast, and led his men in the fight against the Western Allies in Normandy. He was eventually captured and finished the war as a POW, but his spirit was unbroken – famously he escaped the camp where he was held prisoner in Mississippi, USA, just to post a letter in a local post office without it being censored by the camp guards, and then, after a stroll in town and a nice meal, he returned to camp.

Cost: 175pts (Veteran)
Team: 1 officer and up to 2 other men
Weapons: Submachine gun, assault rifle, pistol or rifle/carbine as depicted on the model
Options:
- Ramcke may be accompanied by up to 2 men at a cost of +14pts per man.

Special Rules:
- Stubborn (see the *Fallschirmjäger* Reinforced Platoon on page 36, and note that Ramcke and the men in his team don't have to pay the additional point to upgrade to Stubborn – they already are!).
- Lead by example: Ramcke's Morale bonus is +4 and the range of his ability is 12".
- Behind enemy lines: if Ramcke is in your force, all Outflanking units from the *Fallschirmjäger* Reinforced Platoon ignore the –1 modifier to the Order Test for coming onto the table.

OPERATION *TORCH* AND TUNISIA

The 10th Panzer Division at El Guettar, Dawn, 23 March 1943, by Michael Welply © Osprey Publishing Ltd. Taken from Campaign 152: Kasserine Pass 1943.

America's eventual entry into the World War II was the lifeline that the British desperately needed. However, the initial plan, favoured by General George Marshal, US Army Chief of Staff, was for an immediate invasion of France, bulldozing through northern Europe straight for Berlin. Churchill recoiled at the idea – Hitler had begun fortifying the French coast with formidable beach defences, and three British attempts at securing a foothold on European soil, in Norway, Greece and at Dieppe, had abjectly failed. Churchill persuaded President Roosevelt that the best way of weakening the German grip on Europe was to attack first the 'soft underbelly' – Italy. Mussolini's armies had already demonstrated that they were too ill-equipped and badly led to withstand against the British in North Africa. An invasion of Italy had a good chance of toppling Mussolini from power and laying bare the frontiers of Germany from the south. But first, North Africa had to be secured. Rommel was already on the run back to his base of operations in Libya. The surest chance of finishing him off was to trap him in a vice between Montgomery's cautiously advancing Eighth Army in the east and American forces invading from the west.

Sherman III

The territories at Rommel's western flank, Morocco and Algeria, were held by Colonial French forces loyal to the Vichy regime, which was allowed by the Germans to control central and southern France as the result of a policy of appeasement and collaboration with its Nazi overlords. The American invasion of these territories was codenamed Operation *Torch*.

OPERATION *TORCH*

The Americans assumed that the French in these colonies would readily switch their allegiance to the Allies and allow the invasion force to land unopposed. However, they had seriously misjudged the deep mistrust the French had of the British. The generals and admirals of Vichy France despised the British for their sinking of the French fleet, harboured at Mers-el-Kebir in French Algeria, to stop it from falling into the hands of the Reich. As allies of the British, the Americans had no hope of winning over the French. Where diplomacy failed, the Americans attempted to oust the Vichy top brass in Algeria with a coup organised by their top diplomat there, Robert Murphy, but this came to nothing.

On 8 November 1942, three American armies, accompanied by a few British brigades and units of British commandos, and transported by a fleet of the Royal Navy, approached the shores of Vichy controlled North Africa. Western Task Force, with 33,000 troops commanded by Major General George Patton, aimed for Casablanca in French Morocco. Further east, in French Algeria, Center Task Force, with 35,000 men led by Major General Lloyd Fredendall, would attack the port of Oran, while the objective of Eastern Task Force, comprising of 39,000 men led by Major General Charles Ryder, was the capital, Algiers. The landings were unopposed – the Vichy French and the German high command assumed that the ships massed near Gibraltar were heading either to reinforce Malta or to attack the Germans in Tunisia, and so German submarines concentrated along the coast of Tunisia, too far east to be any danger.

Two hours after the Allied landings, a small force of Americans approached Oran by sea, offering an olive branch and hoping to be allowed to disembark peacefully. Their mission was to forestall any attempted destruction of the port's vital facilities. It was eradicated almost to a man by shellfire from the coastal forts. A similar mission against Algiers fared little better. The message was clear – the French intended to resist.

However, the French were outnumbered and outgunned by the invaders. The initial landings took the French by surprise and were met by sporadic and ineffectual resistance. The defenders, who included many colonial troops such as Senegalese riflemen, were poorly armed and equipped. The 26th Infantry, for example, landing near Oran was counter-attacked by a handful of obsolete Renault tanks that took only 15 minutes to destroy. Virtually unopposed, the Allied forces had gained a first foothold in North Africa.

The opening moves of Operation *Torch* also saw the first US airborne assault, as paratroopers were flown from Cornwall to seize two airfields outside Oran. The mission failed completely. They had not trained for night-time operations, and bad weather scattered the planes. It was an inauspicious start to the invasion.

Such disorganisation and chaos plagued the amphibious landings too. Landing craft were overloaded and sunk, units landed on the wrong beaches or arrived late. Snipers and the

Slowly and methodically, the Afrika Korps clears a settlement.

odd machine-gun crew accounted for many American soldiers, too green to keep their heads down.

On the other hand, Algiers fell easily. Admiral Darlan, the Vichy commander-in-chief, and General Juin, commanding only 7,000 poorly armed troops, were surrounded by 30,000 soldiers and blockaded by British warships. The Luftwaffe, flying from bases in Italy, made a foray against a group of transports at anchor near Algiers, sinking the USS *Leedstown*, but this was just a minor setback. Darlan quickly surrendered Algiers to the Allies, but had no authority to order a cease-fire beyond the city.

The troops converging on Oran had a tougher time of it. Guarding the town of St. Cloud on the main road into Oran from the east was the 16th Tunisian Infantry Regiment, the 1st Battalion of the Foreign Legion, an artillery battalion and a unit of French fascists – the *Service d'Ordre*

*Major General
George S. Patton*

Legionnaire. They put up a stubborn resistance, seeing off attacks by the US 18th Infantry until unleashing their artillery, which stopped the Americans in their tracks. The 18th Infantry, reinforced, attacked again the next morning, sustaining heavy casualties and failing to take the French positions. In the end, the Americans simply bypassed St. Cloud, leaving a holding force to deter the town's defenders from attacking the Americans in the rear. Now Oran was completely surrounded. On 10 November, the port surrendered, but not until much of the harbour area had been sabotaged and ships scuttled to prevent the Allies using them. St. Cloud resisted for another five hours, only falling after vicious house to house fighting. Major General Terry Allen, who commanded the forces around Oran, refused to use artillery to flush the defenders out for fear of massacring the civilians trapped in the town.

barrage from the 30th Infantry Regiment pummelled troops defending a coastal battery a few miles north-east of Fedala, and a bombardment from the US Navy finished the job, but not before the ships managed to land a few shells amongst friendly troops.

The march from Fedala to Casablanca was delayed by a lack of supplies caused by utter confusion on the landing beaches. Guns were unloaded with no ammunition, while vital medical supplies and radio equipment remained unloaded. By the first light of 10 November, Patton was still five miles from his objective.

Patton's attack on Casablanca was scheduled for the morning of 11 November. To secure a base for his airpower, Patton had sent Brigadier General Lucian Truscott with 9,000 troops to capture the coastal town of Mehdia, 80 miles north of Casablanca. Mehdia was protected by an old fortress, known as the Kasbah to the Americans, and manned by 3,000 colonial French defenders. On 8 November, following an unopposed landing, American soldiers attacked the Kasbah, but were driven off by its 85 defenders, who were soon reinforced by 200 others. The fort could not simply be bypassed, as its artillery could pepper any force attempting to invest Mehdia. The French counter-attacked with three Renault tanks, which, despite their poor state of repair, routed the American 2nd Battalion, until then untested in battle. Throughout the night, the Americans were sniped at and suffered bombardment from the fort's guns with no chance of reply as the American artillery had not yet been disembarked. On 9 November, Truscott attacked again, and the Americans and French became locked in a tank battle between the handful of American light tanks that had landed and the decrepit French Renaults. With support from the cruiser *Savannah*, which repulsed a force of French armoured reinforcements, the Americans gradually secured their landing site. Dawn the next day saw 75 American commandos land from the USS *Dallas* and capture Mehdia's airfield in a lightning raid. But the Kasbah refused to yield. Running short of supplies, Truscott launched a final attack, which was initially repulsed until a pair of 105mm guns were dragged to the walls and fired point-blank. A bombardment by

With Algiers and Oran in Allied hands, only Morocco remained under Vichy control. The French navy chose to make a stand at Casablanca, supported by the coastal battery at El Hank. The US Navy and American fighter-bombers destroyed the French ships and ravaged the ships in anchor at Casablanca's harbour. The remnants of the French fleet slunk away, having barely scratched the American ships.

Meanwhile, Patton landed unopposed at Fedala, 10 miles south of Casablanca. Seven hours earlier, the US Navy and an amphibious force of the 47th Infantry Regiment had seized the port of Safi. The capture of the harbour here allowed the easy disembarkation of Patton's 54 Sherman tanks, which would make the 140 mile journey to Casablanca overland to outflank the city from the south, avoiding its coastal guns. As with the landings in Algeria, Patton's troops were scattered, disorganised, for 40 miles across the coastline. But as with the Task Forces further east, Patton's force heavily outnumbered the 2,500 defenders and their 46 artillery pieces. A mortar

Panzerjäger I tank destroyer

a squadron of Navy dive-bombers finished the task – the American infantry finally breached the defences and the Kasbah at last fell.

With Mehdia's capture, Casablanca's defenders now faced enemies from north and south. At dawn on 11 November, with Patton's infantry and tanks edging closer to the city, his guns trained on their targets and Navy dive-bombers already in the air, the French capitulated. After three days of fighting, Vichy control of French Morocco and French Algeria was no more. American casualties amounted to over 2,200 men, not a high figure in comparison with the battles to come, but casualties that would have been saved had the French decided not to obstinately resist for the sake of honour.

Had the Americans faced a more determined enemy, they might have been pushed back into the sea. The American troops were inexperienced and untested on the field of battle. Churchill had been right to divert the American war effort away from northern France – it could have been a massacre. At least the Americans had been bloodied in relatively easy victories, and the lessons learned from the troubled amphibious landings would prove vital for the subsequent landings in Italy and, ultimately, Normandy.

Hitler's response to the American invasion was to occupy southern France with German troops, in case the Allies attempted to liberate France from the Mediterranean. The Vichy government had failed utterly in its goal to maintain at least some French sovereignty. Hitler also hastened the construction of the Atlantic Wall, diverting desperately needed resources and manpower from the Eastern Front.

The Afrika Korps were now penned in Western Libya and Eastern Tunisia, threatened on both flanks. With Gibraltar secured following the capture of the major Algerian and Moroccan ports, the Axis supply lines across the Mediterranean were now even more unstable. Rommel's position in North Africa did not look promising.

Rommel's forces move out.

Panzer III Ausf M

TUNISIA

By the time the Vichy French in North Africa had been defeated, Rommel had moved troops and aircraft into French Tunisia, flagrantly breaking the Armistice conditions of 1940. Hitler was forced to reinforce Rommel's position with troops who would have been crucial to the fight on the Eastern Front, but he could not afford to see North Africa used as a staging post for the invasion of Southern Europe.

As a consequence, the Allied advance towards Tunis, capital of Tunisia, marched into hostile territory. The Allied vanguard consisted of the British 1st Army, accompanied

by several American armoured units and a few Free French infantry battalions, all commanded by Lieutenant General Kenneth Anderson. He split his already small force into four, and each splinter was ambushed in the rain-lashed rugged hills west of Tunis by German forces, mainly paratrooper battalions supported by 88mm guns, panzers, and Stuka dive-bombers. On 3 December, the newly arrived 10th Panzer Division, which included a few of the new Tiger tanks, mauled Anderson's troops, pushing them back.

To protect against the oncoming 8th Army in the east, Rommel mustered a line of defence at Mersa al Brega on the Gulf of Sirte, which had been the starting point of his campaign in February 1942. The 8th Army was progressing slowly and methodically across the Libyan Desert. Montgomery was very wary that a sudden German counter-attack might undo all he

had won at El Alamein, conscious of the cycle of victories and defeats that the British had so far endured in North Africa. The only units far enough forward to trouble the retreating Afrika Korps were the armoured cars of the Royal Dragoons and 11th Hussars.

Rommel abandoned the Mersa al Brega line later in December, defying a direct order from Hitler to stand and defend it to the last. In fact, Rommel was convinced that he was now fighting an impossible battle, and advocated withdrawing the entire Afrika Korps to defend Italy against Allied attack. Instead, Hitler continued to funnel reinforcements into Tunisia, which merely exacerbated the Germans' fuel and ammunition supply problems.

KASSERINE PASS

On 23 January 1943, the 8th Army at last occupied Tripoli. Rommel had again retreated, fortifying the Mareth Line near the Bay of Gabes, where he joined up with the Fifth Panzer Army of *Generaloberst* von Arnim. The two forces were in danger from the American II Corps approaching from the south. To prevent the Americans from traversing the mountains through the Kasserine Pass, which would separate Arnim's tanks from Rommel's army, the 5th Panzers, supported by the 21st Panzer Division, tried to secure the area by attempting to wrest the Faid Pass from a poorly equipped French force on 30th January. The French called upon the Americans for aid, but General Fredenhall, commander of the II Corps, was slow to respond. By the time his troops arrived, the rocky pass was firmly in German hands. The US 1st Armoured Division was the first to counter-attack, but were in turn ambushed by concealed 88mm guns, which pulverised over half the force. The survivors fled, leaving Sherman tanks burning behind them. The Americans tried again, but again sustained heavy casualties from the far more experienced German troops.

Fredenhall, commanding from far behind the lines, and unaware of conditions at the front, sent forward several waves of uncoordinated attacks with inexperienced troops, each of which was easily repulsed by the Germans. After two weeks of fending off the inconsequential Allied attacks, on 14 February Rommel went on the offensive. The 10th Panzer Division attacked westwards from the Faid Pass, while the 21st Panzer Division made an outflanking manoeuvre from the south. The two sides clashed at Sidi Bou Zid, where 70 American tanks were obliterated during the first day's fighting. The monstrous German Tiger tank proved a fearsome adversary, with its 88mm gun and front armour that proved impenetrable to the Shermans' shells, even at close range.

The following day, a Sherman battalion from the 1st Armoured Division was wiped out as it counter-attacked, and an Afrika Korps detachment seized the town of Gafsa, after the Americans holding it hurriedly abandoned it. Rommel's Panzers advanced through the night to Sbeitla, but were held up the next day by a stout defence by American units that had

The charge of the 2/1st Armored at Sidi Bou Zid, 15 February 1943, by Michael Welply © Osprey Publishing Ltd. Taken from Campaign 152: Kasserine Pass 1943.

8th Army infantry section

rallied. Most of their compatriots fled before Rommel's force, however, and on 20th, the American line collapsed – even on the brink of defeat the Desert Fox could snatch a major victory. But the Kasserine Pass was to be his final triumph. The German advance was blocked by Anglo-American reinforcements guarding the roads to Sbiba and Thala, and

American artillery, skilfully manned, forced Rommel to abandon his attack. Thick cloud had suppressed the Allies' advantage in airpower for the last few weeks, but now the skies cleared and Rommel had little protection against the Allied planes.

THE AFRIKA KORPS DEFEATED

Rommel returned to the Mareth Line on 23 February, having wreaked carnage against the Allies – Fredenhall's II Corps had lost over 6,000 men, 180 tanks, 100 half-tracks, 200 field guns and 500 transport vehicles. But these were losses that the Americans, with their superior rates of production, could quickly recoup. And Rommel's victory was soon overshadowed by the disaster of Operation *Oxhead*, where Arnim attacked the British on 26 February, in an assault planned without Rommel's knowledge, which resulted in heavy casualties and

the loss of most of the Arnim's panzers.

With Rommel's star fading in Hitler's eyes, and overall command of the Afrika Korps reverting to the Italian *Comando Supremo* for the sake of Axis unity, Rommel was ordered to hold the Mareth Line, no matter what. He launched a final attack against the 8th Army, in a vain attempt to unbalance the major offensive that Rommel knew Montgomery was planning. But the British knew exactly what Rommel's plans were, thanks once again to Ultra, and, on 6 March, Rommel's forces

The Afrika Korps on the move

Sherman tanks from the 8th Armoured Brigade advance through Wilder's Gap during the New Zealand Corps' operation to outflank the Mareth Line, by Steve Noon © Osprey Publishing Ltd. Taken from Campaign 250: The Mareth Line 1943.

advanced into a trap, where the British tanks, anti-tank guns and artillery made short work of them. The Germans, utterly unaware that their secrets were being decoded, blamed Italian subterfuge for the obvious leak of their battle plans.

Exhausted and ill, Rommel returned to Germany for treatment on 9 March. With the master architect of the Axis victories in North Africa gone, the command of the American II

Corps was strengthened by Eisenhower's sacking of the incompetent Fredenhall and his replacement with Patton, promoted to a three star lieutenant general, who tightened the discipline and improved the morale of his troops, still dazed from their humiliation at Kasserine. Although Patton was ordered to threaten the flank of the southernmost Axis army (now renamed the First Italian Army) in order to support the

victory achieved by the US Army against a German force, and a major morale booster after the tragedy at Kasserine.

On 20 March, Montgomery sent the XXX Corps against the Mareth Line, hoping that the New Zealanders under Freyberg, supported by tanks, would dislodge the enemy with an outflanking manoeuvre from the south-west. The initial frontal attack by the 50th Division was a disaster – the Axis could still hold their own in an equal fight. But when, on 26 March, the armoured brigades of X Corps reinforced the New Zealanders behind the Mareth Line, and the 4th Indian Division was also sent in, the Axis line faltered. At the Tebaga Gap, the weak Axis defences were broken, but the First Italian Army made a rapid withdrawal to Tunis, escaping Montgomery's clutches. The retreating Germans and Italians were closely pursued by the Desert Air Force, which whittled down their numbers with sortie after sortie.

On 7 April, the forward units of the 8th and 1st Armies met up, and by the beginning of May, a quarter of a million Axis troops were boxed in within the northern tip of Tunisia. Almost half of these troops were German, and the rest Italian, most of whom were not fit to fight. Ammunition and fuel, as ever, were dangerously low. Hitler refused to evacuate this force, demanding that they fight to the last man. Indeed, he continued to send reinforcements to the region up until the very end. The Luftwaffe's transport planes were ambushed by the Allied aircraft – over half of Germany's aerial transport capability was shot down over Tunisia in the final two months of the campaign.

The Axis was still capable of meting out some punishment, however – Montgomery suffered heavy losses while attempting to subdue the mountainous Enfidaville sector on the coast south of Tunis. The 8th Army were veterans at desert warfare, but the highland terrain they faced in Tunisia proved a challenge. Further west, the 1st Army also faced stiff resistance. Nevertheless, the American II Corps, west of Tunis, made significant gains.

Changing tactics, Montgomery now concentrated his forces and launched Operation *Strike* on 6 May – a final hammer blow that split the enemy pocket in two. The 7th Armoured Division, 4th Indian Division and 201st Guards Battalion attacked from the south-west, following an intensive artillery barrage that shattered the enemy morale. Simultaneously, the Americans seized Bizerta on the north coast. On 12th May, the Allies entered Tunis, and the Axis generals surrendered. Hitler lost 250,000 Axis troops who would have been invaluable in the subsequent defence of Italy had he listened to Rommel's advice. With the entire North African littoral now in Allied hands, the way was clear for the invasion of Sicily, the stepping stone to mainland Italy, and, as far as Churchill was concerned at least, the key to the destruction of fascist power in southern Europe.

British 8th Army's advance, he couldn't abide Montgomery taking all the glory, and pushed his force forward, retaking Gafsa and securing the Eastern Dorsale massif, which provided strategic control over the coastal plain. Patton's 1st Infantry Division held on to the high ground at El Guettar, resisting an attack by the 10th Panzer Division and destroying half the division's tanks in a savage battle – it was the first significant

FIGHTING OPERATION *TORCH* USING *BOLT ACTION*

Operation *Torch* gives you the opportunity to field American troops for the first time on your North African gaming table. It also allows you the unique opportunity to play World War II battles involving French and American troops on opposing sides.

Although the landings were generally lightly opposed, and American strength in numbers and materiel quickly subdued the Vichy colonies, there were a few instances where green US troops faced a challenge from defenders determined to uphold the honour of France. It is these actions that make the best source for *Bolt Action* games set during this operation.

There were three major objectives for Operation *Torch*: The Western Task Force, commanded by Major General George S. Patton, was to take Casablanca. The Center Task Force, led by Major General Lloyd Fredendall, aimed at Oran, and Algiers was the target of the Eastern Task Force. Although commanded by the British officer, Lieutenant-General Kenneth Anderson, the landing at Algiers was commanded on the field by Major General Charles Ryder of the US Army, because it was considered that the French would be less likely to surrender to the British. British troops were involved in the Eastern Task Force, alongside their US allies, but wore US uniforms to avoid French antagonism.

THEATRE SELECTORS

The following theatre selectors should be used to represent the forces involved in Operation *Torch*.

Valentine tank

USA
- Operation *Torch* Reinforced Platoon (*Armies of the United States*, page 55)

GREAT BRITAIN
- Tunisia Reinforced Platoon (*Armies of Great Britain*, page 75) – representing the British in the Eastern Task Force, though to be historically accurate, you should use US models to represent the infantry.
- Raiders Reinforced Platoon (*Armies of Great Britain*, page 69) – representing the Commandos who participated in the landings at Algiers.

VICHY FRENCH
- Defence of Vichy Reinforced Platoon (*Armies of France and the Allies*, page 36).

OPERATION *TORCH* SPECIAL RULES
The following special rules are pertinent to battles fought in this campaign:

MULTINATIONAL FORCES
The Eastern Task Force lends itself well to the Multinational Forces rules on page 120.

NAVAL GUNS
The landings were fully supported by the offshore guns of the US and Royal Navies. For scenarios that use a Preparatory Bombardment, the bombardment will automatically take place, unless the game is set at Casablanca, where no covering fire heralded the landings under the mistaken belief that the French would surrender without a fight. In this case, no Preparatory Bombardment takes place.

USING CAPTURED ENEMY VEHICLES
During the latter stages of Kasserine, the Germans infiltrated the final defensive positions of the British 26th Armoured Brigade at night using a captured Valentine tank, which caused havoc in the British lines. This would make a splendid little *Bolt Action* scenario, using the rules on page 133.

SCENARIOS
GENERAL SCENARIOS

The following scenarios from the *Bolt Action* rulebook are suitable for the kind of actions that took place during Operation *Torch*.

- Scenario 1: Envelopment (page 108)
- Scenario 2: Maximum Attrition (page 110)
- Scenario 3: Point Defence (page 112)
- Scenario 4: Hold Until Relieved (page 114)

AIRBORNE LANDINGS

Operation *Torch* was the first major airborne assault carried out by the US. The 509th Parachute Infantry Regiment was flown from Britain and, despite terrible weather and poor navigation which scattered the paratroopers, their objectives – the airports at Tafraoui and Es Sénia near Oran, were taken.

To represent these missions, players could agree to use the rules for Airborne Platoons and Combat Jumps on page 126.

AMPHIBIOUS LANDINGS

The Amphibious Invasion scenario detailed below can be used to represent the invasion by sea during Operation *Torch*.

TERRAIN

The battlefield should represent a typical coastline of Morocco or Algeria – sandy beaches leading up to low rocky hills, verdant with scrubland, with perhaps a fishing village nearby with an olive grove or wheat field. A battlefield objective could be a shore battery, such as the one captured by the 1st US Ranger Battalion at Oran.

Alternatively, the game could take place in the port of one of the target cities. There was little resistance to the landings at Algiers, except at the docks, where troops were disembarked to capture key harbour facilities before the French could sabotage them.

Note that Operation *Torch* took place in November, and though the summer months are hot in this region, in winter the weather is cold. The action took place along the fertile coast too, so the Desert Fighting rules don't apply for games set during this operation.

SCENARIO 8: BLOOD ON THE BEACHES – AMPHIBIOUS INVASION

The following scenario is designed to recreate one of the few instances of resistance at the beach landings during Operation *Torch*. It can also be adapted to represent a beach landing in any World War II theatre.

Note that for the Operation *Torch* landings, the beaches are unfortified or lightly fortified, and the attacking Allies gain the benefit of the Naval Guns rule described above. The Desert Warfare rules are not used for this scenario, as it takes place on the coast.

FORCES

This scenario is designed to be played with equal points values on both sides. The following reinforced platoons should be used to represent the forces involved:

USA

- Operation *Torch* Reinforced Platoon (*Armies of the United States*, page 55)

BRITISH & COMMONWEALTH

- Tunisia Reinforced Platoon (*Armies of Great Britain*, page 75) – representing the British in the Eastern Task Force.
- Raiders Reinforced Platoon (*Armies of Great Britain*, page 69) – representing the Commandos who participated in the landings at Algiers.

VICHY FRENCH

- Defence of Vichy Reinforced Platoon (*Armies of France and the Allies*, page 36).

Commando Vickers MMG team

SET-UP

TERRAIN

From the attacker's point of view, the first 12" of the table from the defender's edge consists of deep water, the next 12" is shallow water, then 12" of beach (rough ground) and the last 12" is where the defender deploys his units and fortifications (if any).

DEPLOYMENT

The defending player places half of his forces (rounding up), within 12" of his table edge – this is his deployment area. They may start the game hidden)

If the beach is unfortified, no fortifications are placed. If it is lightly fortified, a few obstacles, such as barbed wire, low walls, sandbag emplacements, tank traps or ditches, and up to one bunker, can be placed by the defender in his deployment area.

If the beach is heavily fortified, the defender can place many fortifications in his deployment area. In addition, he gets one minefield section (see page 131) per landing craft used by the attackers, and can place these plus a good number of obstacles that are impassable to vehicles anywhere on the beach and/or water areas.

Any units not deployed are held back in reserve.

The attacking player places no units at the start of the game. Instead he must nominate at least half his force as his first wave. Any units not included in the first wave are held back in reserve.

SPECIAL RULES

PREPARATORY BOMBARDMENT

The attacker automatically gets a preparatory bombardment against the enemy positions (see *Bolt Action*, page 118).

FIRST TURN

During Turn 1, the attacking player must bring his entire first wave onto the table. These units can enter from any point on the attacker's table edge. Note that no order test is required to move units onto the table as part of the first wave.

AMPHIBIOUS ASSAULTS

This scenario uses the Amphibious Assaults rule (page 134).

MINEFIELDS

If the area is heavily fortified, the Minefields rules (page 131).

OBJECTIVE

The attacking player must try to move as many of his units as he can into the defender's set-up zone and destroy the defending forces to establish a beachhead. The defending player must try and stop him. Note that in this scenario, attacking units are allowed to deliberately move off the table from the defending player's table edge to reach their objective.

GAME DURATION

Keep a count of how many turns have elapsed as the game is played. At the end of Turn 9, roll a die. On a result of 1, 2 or 3, the game ends, on a roll of 4, 5 or 6 play one further turn.

VICTORY!

At the end of the game, calculate which side has won by adding up victory points as follows. If one side scores at least 2 more victory points than the other then that side has won a clear victory. Otherwise the result is deemed too close to call and the result is a draw!

The attacking player scores 1 victory point for every enemy unit destroyed. He also scores 1 victory point for each of his own units that ends the game in the enemy deployment area and 2 victory points for each of his own unit that has moved off the enemy table edge before the end of the game.

The defending player scores 1 victory point for every enemy unit destroyed.

FIGHTING THE TUNISIAN CAMPAIGN USING BOLT ACTION

With the collapse of the Vichy French in Morocco and Algeria, and with the 8th Army cautiously gaining ground westwards through Libya, the Afrika Korps found itself increasingly penned in from both flanks. Use the following suggestions to play games set during this stage of the North African campaign.

TANK BATTLES

The lowland regions of Tunisia make good terrain for tank battles, so feel free to use the *Tank War* book to pit Axis and Allied armour against each other.

THEATRE SELECTORS

GERMANS

• Rommel's Defeat Reinforced Platoon (*Armies of Germany*, page 79).

ITALIANS

• War in Africa Reinforced Platoon (*Armies of Italy and the Axis*, page 31).

USA

• Kasserine Pass Reinforced Platoon (*Armies of the United States*, page 57) – represents a US force up to and including the disaster at Kasserine Pass (late February 1943).
• El Guettar Reinforced Platoon (*Armies of the United States*, page 58) – represents a US force around the time of the battle of El Guettar (late March 1943).
• Rommel's Defeat Reinforced Platoon (*Armies of the United States*, page 59) – represents a US force up during the last stages of the Tunisian campaign (from early April to early May 1943).

BRITISH & COMMONWEALTH

• Tunisia Reinforced Platoon (*Armies of Great Britain*, page 75).
• Indian Division Reinforced Platoon (page 23).
• Behind Enemy Lines Reinforced Platoon (*Armies of Great Britain*, page 73) – For battles fought in Tunisia, you can choose SAS Infantry Squads (see page 59).

FREE FRENCH

• Free French Reinforced Platoon (page 19) – representing the Free French fighting alongside the main Allied armies (see page 120).

TUNISIAN CAMPAIGN SPECIAL RULES

The following special rules are pertinent to battles fought in this campaign:

HARSH CONDITIONS

For games set in the centre (such as Kasserine Pass or El Guettar) or South of Tunisia, see the rules for Desert Warfare, on page 121. However, note that the fighting took place during the Tunisian winter and early spring, when cold, often windy weather prevails, banishing the stifling heat of summer. Up in the mountains, the troops faced sometimes freezing conditions. This means that the 'Hot, Damned Hot' special Desert Warfare rule is ignored for battles set in the Tunisian campaign, and the weather effects, Haze and Mirage, count as a 'Something's brewing on the horizon' result instead – this makes it slightly more likely that a sandstorm might turn up on the battlefield, which reflects the tempestuous nature of the Tunisian winter.

The Axis forces, British and Commonwealth troops and forces of the Free French that fight in the south are masters in desert warfare – all Regular and Veteran units in these forces gain the Desert Fighters rule for free (see page 122). Inexperienced units can be upgraded with the rule for +2pts each.

American units have to purchase the Desert Fighters rule for +2pts each, but only during battles set after Kasserine Pass. Before then, they are inexperienced in desert combat so cannot utilise that rule.

SCENARIOS

GENERAL SCENARIOS

All scenarios from the *Bolt Action* rulebook are suitable for the kind of actions that took place during the Tunisian campaign.

• Scenario 1: Envelopment (page 108)
• Scenario 2: Maximum Attrition (page 110)
• Scenario 3: Point Defence (page 112)
• Scenario 4: Hold Until Relieved (page 114)
• Scenario 5: Top Secret (page 115)
• Scenario 6: Demolition (page 116)

In addition, special scenarios detailed below allow you to play out the Battle of Kasserine Pass, the Battle of El Guettar, and the fight for Longstop Hill.

TERRAIN

The terrain in Tunisia is different from the flat expanse of sand that is the Libyan and Egyptian deserts to the east. The north of the country comprises of mountainous highland, while a hot, dry plain dominates the centre of the region. It was these types of terrain that the US armies had to conquer while marching east from Algeria.

The semi-arid south of the country merges with the Sahara, and for the initial stages of the Tunisian campaign, the British 8th Army faced similar terrain to that they had experienced in Libya.

SCENARIO 9: CARNAGE AT KASSERINE PASS

The Battle of Kasserine Pass was Rommel's last great achievement in North Africa. It was also the first big engagement between US and German forces. Rommel slaughtered the inexperienced, badly led American troops, pushing them back over 80km from their original positions. It was only stiff resistance from the British at Thala, along with dwindling supplies, that forced Rommel to withdraw. The Americans were bloodied, but certainly not beaten. The survivors emerged toughened and experienced from their ordeal, and the American high command learned valuable lessons from this defeat.

The following scenario focuses on an action that took part during the early stages of the battle, when the Axis troops were trying to break through the pass.

FORCES

This scenario is designed to be played with equal points values on both sides. The following reinforced platoons should be used to represent the forces involved:

GERMANS

• Rommel's Defeat Reinforced Platoon (*Armies of Germany*, page 79).

ITALIANS

• War in Africa Reinforced Platoon (*Armies of Italy and the Axis*, page 31) – the Centauro Division armoured battalion and the 5th *Bersaglieri* saw action at Kasserine. The multinational rules are ideal to represent the various elements of the Afrika Korps present in this scenario.

USA

• Kasserine Pass Reinforced Platoon (*Armies of the United States*, page 57). Note that you have to choose an Engineer squad and at least two other Infantry squads for this scenario. The US side is defending in this scenario.

Note: All Axis units have the Desert Fighters rule. No American units have this rule.

SET-UP

TERRAIN

The battlefield should be set up as shown on the scenario map.

The battlefield is split into three areas: two highland areas on the flanks and an area representing the pass in the centre. As many hills, rocks and boulders as possible should be placed in the two highland areas. No terrain is placed in the pass itself.

Exactly 12" from the table middle line, on the US side of the table, the US player must set up a line of obstacles (sandbags, barbed wire, etc.) across the pass (but not into the highland areas). This is the defensive line constructed by a unit of US Engineers to block the pass.

The defenders also place their minefields at the same time as setting up the obstacles (see the scenario special rules below).

The defenders can also position one 6"x6" emplacement in each of the highland areas on his side of the table, up to the middle line. Each emplacement should be big enough to be occupied by a single infantry or artillery unit, but no bigger.

Note that the rocky ground here is too hard for units to dig in, so the Dug-in rules cannot be used.

DEPLOYMENT

The defender sets up the Engineer squad within his set-up zone, on the pass area. He then sets up one Infantry squad in each emplacement. He then places up to half his remaining units anywhere within his set-up zone. Units not set up to start with are left in reserve.

The attacker's units are not set up on the table at the start of the game. The attacker must nominate at least half of his force to form his first wave. This can be his entire army if he wishes. Any units not included in the first wave are left in reserve.

US 50cal HMG team

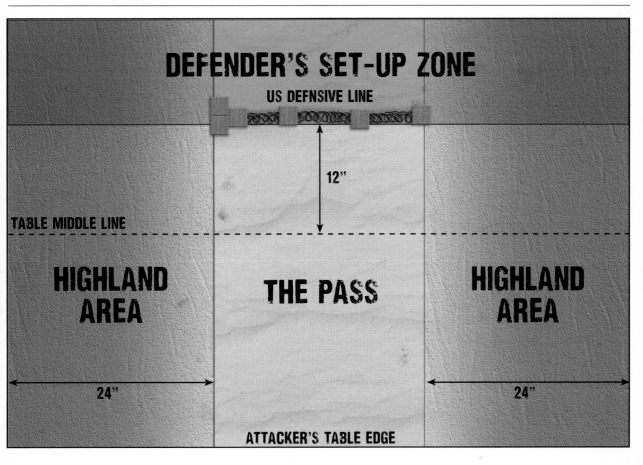

SPECIAL RULES

FIRST TURN

During Turn 1, the attacking player must move his entire first wave onto the table. These units can enter the table from any point on the attacker's table edge, and must be given either a *run* or *advance* order. Note that no order test is required to move units onto the table as part of the first wave.

MULTINATIONAL FORCES

The Axis forces can be a mix of German and Italian units. Refer to the rules on page 120 if you want to field multinational forces.

DESERT WARFARE

This scenario is set in the desert. See the rules for Desert Warfare, on page 121. However, remember that the Dug-In rules cannot be used.

DESERT FIGHTERS

All units on the Axis side have the Desert Fighters special rule (page 122) for free. No American units have this rule.

MINEFIELDS

The defender has one minefield section plus two dummy mines section per full 1,000 points of his force. Plenty of mines had been delivered to the Americans defending the pass, but they had arrived so late that they were hastily laid. Attacking units are only hit by minefields on a 5+, even if they are Inexperienced or Regular.

DISORGANISED DEFENDERS

The defenders are badly led, and suffer from poor communication. Reserves require an order check with a −2 penalty to move onto the table. The US special rule Modern Communications does not apply in this scenario.

RESERVES

The defender's units can only enter the table from their table edge, along the central area representing the pass.

The attacker's units can only enter the table from their table edge, along the central area representing the pass.

Neither side can use outflanking manoeuvres during this scenario.

OBJECTIVE

The attacker must try to move as many of units as he can into the defender's set-up zone or off the defender's table edge. The defender must try to stop him. Note that in this scenario, attacking units are allowed to deliberately move off the table from the defender's table edge to reach their objective.

GAME DURATION

Keep a count of how many turns have elapsed as the game is played. At the end of Turn 6, roll a die. On a result of 1, 2 or 3 the game ends, on a roll of 4, 5 or 6 play one further turn.

SCENARIO 10: THE BATTLE OF EL GUETTAR

In contrast with Kasserine, El Guettar was a great, indeed the first, American victory against the Axis forces. The inept Fredendall, commander at Kasserine, had been replaced by the formidable Patton, and US tactics adapted quickly in response to the defeat.

El Guettar took place on 23 March 1943. A group of Panzers and Panzergrenadiers mounted in half-tracks from the 10th Panzer Division made a daylight attack along the Gabes to Gafsa road, followed by more infantry in trucks. When the Germans were slowed by a minefield, US tank destroyers and intense artillery bombardment forced the attackers to regroup behind a ridgeline, where they waited for the Luftwaffe to soften the blocking enemy force. The air strike achieved little, and when the attack restarted later that afternoon, the Americans had reinforced their positions. This second advance again faltered, mainly due to the punishing effect of the US artillery.

The following scenario recreates an action fought between German and US forces during the Battle of El Guettar.

FORCES

This scenario is designed to be played with equal points values on both sides. The following reinforced platoons should be used to represent the forces involved:

GERMANS

- Rommel's Defeat Reinforced Platoon (*Armies of Germany*, page 79) – the entire force has to be motorised (i.e. the platoon must include enough transport vehicles to transport all infantry and artillery units).

VICTORY!

At the end of the game, calculate which side has won by adding up victory points as follows. If one side scores at least 2 more victory points than the other then that side has won a clear victory. Otherwise the result is deemed too close to call and honours are shared – a draw!

The attacking player scores 1 victory point for every enemy unit destroyed. He also scores 2 victory points for each of his own units that is inside the defender's set-up zone (even if only partially), and 3 victory points for each of his own units that has moved off the enemy table edge before the end of the game.

The defending player scores 2 victory points for every enemy unit destroyed.

USA

- El Guettar Reinforced Platoon (*Armies of the United States*, page 58) – to represent their advantage in artillery, the American player can field a free regular Forward Artillery Observer in addition to any purchased normally.

SET-UP

TERRAIN

A road bisects the table, running from the middle of the attacker's long table edge to the middle of the opposite defender's edge. Like all roads in this region, this is very poorly maintained, so a vehicle moving along it can only double its move rate on the D6 score of a 4+.

The rest of the table consists of flat, rocky, desert terrain, with a few ridgelines in hilly areas no further than 8" from each short table edge.

DEPLOYMENT

The Americans have the initiative in this encounter, and the German player has to deploy at least half his army first, anywhere within his set-up zone.

The American player then sets up at least half his force anywhere within his own set-up zone. Infantry units can be deployed in any hilly area.

Any units not set up during this stage are left in reserve.

SPECIAL RULES

PREPARATORY BOMBARDMENT
The American artillery proved too much for the Germans. To represent this, the defender can automatically execute a preparatory bombardment before the game begins (see *Bolt Action*, page 118). The American player rolls two dice on the Preparatory Bombardment chart and chooses the best result.

FIRST TURN
The battle begins.

DESERT WARFARE
This scenario is set in the desert. See the rules for Desert Warfare, on page 121.

DESERT FIGHTERS
All units on the Axis side have the Desert Fighters special rule (page 122) for free. Regular and Veteran American units can be given the Desert Fighters rule at a cost of +2pts per man.

MINEFIELDS
The American player has two minefield sections per full 1,000 points of his force. See page 131 for the rules on minefields.

CRUCIFYING ARTILLERY BARRAGE
When the American player rolls on the Artillery Barrage chart (*Bolt Action* page 64), he rolls two dice and chooses the best result.

RESERVES
The attacker's reserves can only enter the table from the attacker's table edge, within the area delineated by his set-up zone.

The defender's reserves can enter the table from any point along the defender's table edge.

Only the defender can use outflanking manoeuvres during this scenario.

OBJECTIVE
Both sides must attempt to destroy the other whilst preserving their own forces.

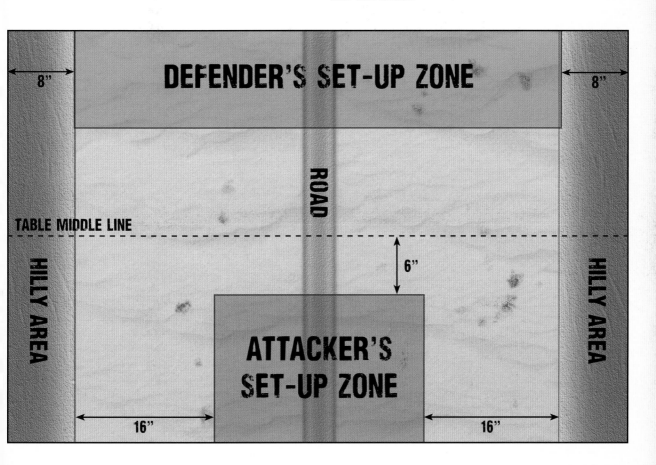

GAME DURATION

Keep a count of how many Turns have elapsed as the game is played. At the end of Turn 6, roll a die. On a result of 1, 2 or 3 the game ends, on a roll of 4, 5 or 6 play one further turn.

VICTORY!

At the end of the game, calculate which side has won by adding up victory points as follows. If one side scores at least 2 more victory points than the other then that side has won a clear victory. Otherwise the result is deemed too close to call and honours are shared – a draw!

Each player scores 1 victory point for every enemy unit destroyed.

8th Army Vickers MMG team

SCENARIO 11: CONTROL THE HEIGHTS – THE CAPTURE OF LONGSTOP HILL

The second battle of Longstop Hill (21–23 April 1943) was fought between British and German forces over the tactically important heights of Djebel el Ahmera and Djebel Rhar, which guarded the road to Tunis, the chief headquarters of the Afrika Korps. After a gruelling battle, the British finally won through, paving the way for an Allied advance on Tunis and total victory in North Africa.

The battle is typical of the bitter hill-to-hill fighting that the Americans and the British had to endure as they clawed their way across the highlands of Tunisia. This scenario can represent any battle where the objective is to push the enemy off well-defended high ground, either in Tunisia or in any other World War II theatre (such as Alpine France and the northern borders of Greece, described earlier in this book.

FORCES

This scenario is designed to be played with equal points values on both sides. The following reinforced platoons should be used to represent the forces involved:

GERMANS

- Rommel's Defeat Reinforced Platoon (*Armies of Germany*, page 79) – the Germans are the defenders in this scenario.

BRITISH & COMMONWEALTH

- Tunisia Reinforced Platoon (*Armies of Great Britain*, page 75) – if tanks are taken, they have to be Churchill tanks; this is the only tank that can cross the rough highland terrain.

SET-UP

TERRAIN

The hill should dominate the centre of the table, but shouldn't be closer than 12" to any table edge. It should be adorned with some hurriedly prepared defences (like sandbag emplacements, dug-outs, etc.).

The defender sets up at least half his force on the hill, no closer than 18" from any table edge. Any units not set up this way are held in reserve.

The attacker does not set up any units at the start of the game. He must nominate at least half his force to form his first wave. Any units not included in the first wave are held back in reserve.

SPECIAL RULES

PREPARATORY BOMBARDMENT

The attacker rolls a die: on a 2+ a preparatory bombardment strikes the enemy positions. On a 1, the barrage fails to materialize, but you have your orders and the attack must go on as planned.

The Afrika Korps traverse the desert.

FIRST TURN

On the first turn, the attacker must bring his entire first wave onto the table. These units can enter the table from any point along either long table edge, and must be given either a *run* or *advance* order. Note that no order test is required to move units onto the table as part of a first wave.

VERY ROUGH GOING

The dry, rocky slopes of Longstop Hill are impassable to all vehicles, except Churchill tanks. For other units, the entire hill counts as rough ground.

OBJECTIVE

The attacker is trying to destroy the forces on the hill. The defender is trying to hold the hill at all costs!

GAME DURATION

Keep a count of how many turns have elapsed as the game is played. At the end of Turn 6, roll a die. On a result of 1, 2 or 3, the game ends, on a roll of 4, 5 or 6 play one further turn.

VICTORY!

At the end of the game calculate which side has won by adding up victory points as follows. If one side scores at least 2 more points than the other then that side has won a clear victory. Otherwise, the result is a draw!

Both players score 1 victory point for every enemy unit destroyed. They also score 1 victory point for each of their units on the hill and within 12" of the table's middle line at the end of the game.

Churchill Mk VIII tank

ADDITIONAL UNITS

GERMANY

999TH LIGHT AFRIKA DIVISION (STRAFBATTALION) SQUAD

The 999th Afrika Brigade was formed in October 1942 as a penal unit in the German Army. It comprised of convicts, whose punishment involved serving in the brigade in lieu of imprisonment or execution. In early 1943, it was expanded into the 999th Light Afrika Division and deployed to North Africa. However, only a few units made it to their posting before the collapse of Axis power in Africa. These briefly fought alongside other elements of the Afrika Korps before its surrender.

Cost: Inexperienced Infantry 35pts or Regular Infantry 50pts
Composition: 1 NCO and 4 men
Weapons: Rifles

Options:
- Add up to 5 additional men with rifles at +4pts each (Inexperienced) or +7pts each (Regular).
- The NCO may have a submachine gun for +3pts.
- Up to 1 man can have a light machine gun for +20pts – another man becomes the loader.

Special Rules:
- *Strafbattalion* can be Shirkers at a cost of –3pts per model

SELECTORS

Strafbattalion count as an infantry squad for the purposes of the generic Reinforced Platoon selector from the *Bolt Action* rulebook. They also count as infantry in a Rommel's Defeat Reinforced Platoon.

THEATRE SELECTORS

THE HERMANN GÖRING DIVISION

The embryo of this division was created in 1933, when Hermann Göring, German Minister of the Interior, formed a police unit utterly dedicated to the Nazi regime. Its members soon gained a reputation for brutally enforcing Nazi ideology. These policemen were militarised in 1934, and transferred to the Luftwaffe when Göring was promoted to command that organisation in 1935. Renamed Regiment General Göring, some of its troops were trained as paratroopers to become the first *Fallschirmjäger* units.

During the opening stages of the war, the regiment saw action everywhere: Poland, Denmark, Norway, the Netherlands, Belgium and France. In 1941 it was restructured as a motorised force, and saw action during Operation *Barbarossa*, where its anti-tank guns became the terror of Soviet armour. The following year, it was transferred to the North African theatre. Now known as the Hermann Göring Division, it saw action only at the rump end of the Tunisian campaign, which saw all its combat units surrender to the Allies following the collapse of the Afrika Korps.

Göring immediately reformed the division and sent it to Sicily, where it fought tenaciously against the invading Allies until forced to retreat to Messina. One of the last units to leave the island, it fought a fierce rearguard, slowing the Allies long enough for the rest of the German army to evacuate unharmed

to the Italian mainland. There, it fought at Salerno, and participated in the gradual fighting retreat to the Gustav Line. Its reputation for brutality followed it, and it was responsible for several reprisals against Italian villages in response to civilian resistance to the occupying German forces.

At Anzio, it resisted the invasion force until the sheer weight of American reinforcements secured the Allied beachhead there. The division forced the Americans to pay a deadly toll in their efforts to cross the Rapido River, and opposed the Allies throughout the early months of 1944 as they pushed towards Rome, again fighting successful delaying actions to ensure the evacuation of German forces from the Eternal City.

In July 1944, the division was transported to the Eastern Front – ultimately, its remnants surrendered to the Soviets in early May 1945. Thus ended a fighting force that had battled in almost every theatre the German army had been involved in.

HERMANN GÖRING DIVISION REINFORCED PLATOON (TUNISIA)

We find that the best way to field a German force to represent the Hermann Göring division for the fighting in Tunisia is to select reinforced platoons from the Rommel's Defeat Reinforced Platoon (*Armies of Germany*, page 79), with the following exceptions:

- The entire force has to be motorised (i.e. the platoon must include enough transport vehicles to transport all infantry and artillery units).
- No units in the force can be purchased as Inexperienced.
- Any Veteran infantry or artillery unit in the force can be upgraded to Fanatics at +3pts per man.
- The 2 mandatory *Heer* Veteran infantry squads in each platoon can be replaced by *Fallschirmjäger* squads (Early War)
- Each platoon can include one additional anti-aircraft gun, which is purchased as normal, amongst the ones listed, but does not count towards the maximum number of artillery units in the platoon (and an additional tow for it, if necessary).
- Each platoon can include an additional anti-aircraft vehicle, which is purchased as normal, amongst the ones listed, but does not count towards the maximum number of vehicles in the platoon.
- All weapons with the flak rule in the force can re-roll their dice when rolling to hit against incoming aircraft during an air strike, as well as when attempting to hold their flak fire against attacking aircraft.

HERMANN GÖRING DIVISION REINFORCED PLATOON (ITALY)

This is the same as for Tunisia, except that the platoons are selected from the Defence of Italy Reinforced Platoon (*Armies of Germany*, page 85). Note that the *Fallschirmjäger* squads need now to be Late War, and that no *Waffen SS* units can be added to the platoons.

HERMANN GÖRING DIVISION ARMOURED PLATOON

You can of course represent the Hermann Göring Division using armoured platoons from *Tank War* rather than normal reinforced platoons. If you decide to do so, select armoured platoons from the Armoured Platoon selector (page 11), with the following exceptions:

- Units in the force must be selected amongst those available either for the Rommel's Defeat selector (for the Hermann Göring Division in Tunisia), or for the Defence of Italy selector (for the Hermann Göring Division in Italy).
- No units in the force can be purchased as Inexperienced.
- Any Veteran infantry or artillery unit in the force can be upgraded to Fanatics at +3pts per man.
- Each platoon can include one additional anti-aircraft gun, which is purchased as normal, amongst the ones listed, but does not count towards the maximum number of artillery units in the platoon (and an additional tow for it, if necessary).
- Each platoon can include an additional anti-aircraft vehicle, which is purchased as normal, amongst the ones listed, but does not count towards the maximum number of vehicles in the platoon.
- All weapons with the flak rule in the force can re-roll their dice when rolling to hit against incoming airplanes during an air strike, as well as when attempting to hold their flak fire against attacking aircraft.

Afrika Korps squad

ITALY INVADED

The battle for Lilienthal, Uncle Beach, by Steve Noon © Osprey Publishing Ltd. Taken from Campaign 257: Salerno 1943

For the British, an invasion of Italy promised many tactical opportunities. If Hitler reinforced Italy with German forces, he would have to withdraw troops from the Eastern Front, easing the pressure on the Russians, or redeploy troops occupying Western Europe, which would benefit the imminent Anglo-American invasion of occupied France. But if the Nazis failed to bolster Italy, and the country fell to the Allies, Mussolini's power would crumble and an Axis nation would be kicked out of the war. The Allies would have complete control of the Mediterranean, shortening the shipping route to the Far East and helping the war effort against the Japanese. Moreover, Churchill had his sights set on the Balkans, with a view of seizing Eastern Europe before Stalin's armies could rumble in and take them in the name of Communism, and a swift conquest of Italy was imperative for this to happen.

However, the Americans were eager to embark on the invasion of occupied France, as had been their intention when they joined the war. Many US generals, including Marshall, still regarded their adventures in the Mediterranean as a sideshow and were eager to forge on to Berlin from the shores of Normandy. However, Churchill persuaded Eisenhower of the benefits that the defeat of Mussolini would bring, and a compromise was reached – assuming that Sicily would swiftly be taken, seven of the US divisions in the Mediterranean would be moved from Sicily to take part in the Normandy invasion planned for the spring of 1944. And so the scene was set for Operation *Husky*, the invasion of Sicily.

Uncle Sam's boys storm into the heart of Italy.

THE INVASION OF SICILY

Before daybreak on 10 July 1943, the Allies initiated the invasion with airdrops near the towns of Gela and Syracuse, followed by an amphibious landing of eight divisions by 2,600 ships. Montgomery's 8th Army was to secure the south-eastern tip of Sicily before heading along the northern coast to capture the port of Messina, the town closest to mainland Italy. Patton's US 7th Army was to seize the western part of the island.

The Axis had been led to believe by Allied misinformation that the invasion's target was to be Sardinia and Greece, and Mussolini had reinforced Sardinia as a result. The 300,000 strong Axis force on Sicily, controlled by the Italian General Guzzoni, were taken by complete surprise, and the Allies landed 80,000 men, 3,000 vehicles, 300 tanks and 900 guns without opposition. There were two German divisions posted on the island, the Hermann Göring Panzer Division, which was close enough to intercept the invaders, and the 15th Panzergrenadiers, which was deployed on the western coast, too far to launch an immediate counter-attack.

It was lucky that the landings were unopposed, as rough seas battered the amphibious craft and many units disembarked far from their planned rendezvous. Little had been learned from the fiasco of the Operation *Torch* landings, and confusion reigned on the beaches as lost soldiers tried to reunite with their divisions and supplies reached the shore in a chaotic fashion.

The airdrops unfolded in a similarly haphazard way. High winds scattered the forces of the British 1st Airborne Division and the US 82nd Airborne in all directions. The British glider force, aiming to secure Ponte Grande, a bridge vital to the Allied plans to capture Syracuse was the most spectacular failure – 60 gliders crashed into the sea, one landed in Malta, and one in Tunisia! Only 30 men managed to reach the target, reinforced by 50 of their comrades later that morning. Nevertheless, they held the bridge against a far superior Italian force for most of the day until forced to surrender. This Axis victory was brief, however, as the Royal Scots Fusiliers, speedily mobilised after their beach landing, retook the bridge soon afterwards.

The morning of 11 July saw the Panzers of the Hermann Göring Division advance against the Americans at the town of Gela on the south coast. The Italian Livorno Division supported the attack, but were pinned by intense mortar fire directed by Patton himself, and by accurate naval gunfire from offshore cruisers and destroyers. The Panzers, however, pushed the Americans almost back to the beach – the American infantry had been caught without tank and artillery support, which were still being transported offshore, and were being ground down by the relentless Panzer advance. At the last minute, the balance tipped to the Americans' favour when a platoon of Shermans and some artillery were landed on the beach and

Rangers lead the way!

swiftly went into action. A devastating naval bombardment finished the job, and the German tanks were forced to withdraw, to the cheers of Patton's men. However, the Americans continued to be harassed by the *Luftwaffe*, strafing and bombing their lines throughout the day – as night settled in, men huddled down nervously scanning the dark skies.

In the early hours of 12 July, the night was suddenly lit up by a blaze of gunfire, and thundered with the roar of anti-aircraft artillery loosing a hellstorm. Overhead, planes spiralled down in flames, while troops parachuting to the ground were torn apart by rifle fire. Patton was aghast. His men were firing on the US 504th Parachute Infantry Regiment flying in from Tunisia to reinforce the 7h Army. He had earlier commanded the anti-aircraft crews to expect the drop, but the orders had failed to get through. Over 50 planes were destroyed or badly damaged that morning, and 400 paratroopers lost to 'friendly fire'. The Allies had yet to master the innovative tactics of deploying troops by air.

While the Americans were reeling from this disaster, the British 8th Army faced stiff resistance as they followed the east coast road to Catania. Montgomery had seized Syracuse with relative ease, but now faced German reinforcements from the mainland: the 29th Panzergrenadiers and the 1st *Fallschirmjäger* paratroop division, commanded by General Hube of the XIV Panzer Corps. The Hermann Göring Panzers were withdrawn from Gela to face the British, relieving Patton of further immediate attacks.

On 13 July, the British attempted to seize the Primosole Bridge crossing the River Simeto near Catania with a drop of the 1st Parachute Brigade. But these too had to run the gauntlet of the Allied fleet, before being pounded by Axis anti-aircraft guns, and only 300 of the 1,800 paratroopers reached the bridge. The following day, they held the bridge against fierce attacks from the *Fallschirmjäger*, grimly holding their objective until the Germans were eventually driven off by an attack from the 151st Brigade supported by the Durham Light Infantry, where the river ran red with British blood. The arrival of the 4th Armoured Brigade finally secured the bridge for the British.

As this bitter fighting took place, the 51st Highlanders was advancing through the Sicilian hills, taking village after village in short, fierce actions. Attempting to seize the airfield at Gerbini, they were torn to shreds by their old nemesis from North Africa, the German 88mm anti-tanks guns. The Hermann Göring and *Fallschirmjäger* divisions forced the British to fight for every ridge, slowing Montgomery's advance. In an attempt to outflank the blocking Germans, Montgomery, with the agreement of General Alexander, swung his XXX Corps around the western side of Mount Etna. But this forced him to encroach on Patton's zone, which incensed the Americans, who were not notified of the manoeuvre. The American and British generals were joined in common purpose... but this didn't mean they had to like each other.

Patton's main frustration was that his forces were simply protecting the British left flank. This would not win him the glory he was so eager for. On 17 July, after a week of inaction, he persuaded Alexander to allow him to take the port of Agrigento on the west coast in order to open up a new supply route. What he didn't tell his superior was that he intended to push his forces further up the coast and north through the mountains towards Palermo, to capture it before Montgomery did. He achieved this on 22 July, his tanks, troop transports and self-propelled artillery sweeping across Sicily meeting little resistance, while the British fought the Axis to a stalemate at the foothills of Mount Etna. The 8th Army, though highly experienced desert fighters, found these battles in the bleak highlands extremely challenging, and the Italian troops were putting up a considerably stiffer resistance to the invasion of their homeland than they had done in the defence of Mussolini's 'empire' in Africa. In one case, a Canadian 1st Division regiment had to scale a cliff to capture the mountaintop town of Assoro. This incessant slogging match against a well-defended foe sapped the morale and the strength of the Allied soldiers, despite Montgomery's chipper assertions that all was going according to plan.

In contrast, Patton's 7th Army forged on to Messina relentlessly, despite the intense heat of the Sicilian summer, dehydration, dysentery and malaria, to which over 20,000 Allied troops would succumb in Sicily. At a meeting in Syracuse on the 25 July, Montgomery agreed to allow Patton to enter the British zone of operations if it meant that Messina would fall quickly to the Allies.

Alexander arrived late at the meeting, delayed by news from the previous day that Mussolini had been arrested at the royal palace of King Vittorio Emanuele III in Rome, and replaced by Marshal Pietro Badoglio as prime minister. The Marshal promised Hitler that the war would continue, but a sceptical Fuhrer immediately seized the Brenner Pass in North Italy with eight divisions, and made plans to occupy the entire country if Italy surrendered. The railyards of Rome and the docks of Naples were now targets for Allied bombing raids, and the will of the Italian people to fight on was paper-thin.

Patton's forces smashed through the Axis troops defending the northern route to Messina with the subtlety of a sledgehammer. The Americans had learned the hard way at Kasserine Pass how to wage war in the highlands, and advanced steadily across the rocky hills, seizing the high ground to force the enemy back. Their artillery and air support left towns in smoking ruins in their wake as they bombed the Axis defenders out of their positions, causing huge civilian casualties as a result. The two Panzergrenadier divisions opposing them made them fight hard, and attempted to disrupt their advance by destroying bridges and leaving mines and booby-traps before they were forced back. This only hardened the Americans further to the rigours of war, and the Seventh Army's advance remained relentless.

Patton was often cavalier with the lives of his soldiers in his haste to reach Messina. Despite the misgivings of his subordinate officers, he persuaded the US Navy to land a battalion behind enemy lines. The men were almost completely destroyed while attempting to secure a hill called Monte Cipolla. Despite this setback, the Axis began to evacuate its forces to the mainland, and over 100,000 troops eventually escaped to defend Italy against the imminent Allied invasion. Had the Allies made a concerted effort by land and air to halt this evacuation and force the surrender of these troops, Italy may well have been the soft underbelly proclaimed by Churchill. The Allies would pay dearly in the forthcoming months for this oversight.

Patton's triumphant troops entered Messina on 17 August. Most importantly to Patton, he had got there before Montgomery. But this achievement had been paid for with almost 9,000 American casualties, while the British had suffered almost 13,000. However, the Allies now had almost total control of the Mediterranean and could bomb Italy at will from Sicilian airfields. Mussolini languished in captivity and Hitler's main Axis partner was teetering on the brink of surrender. Only the straits of Messina, a mere 20km wide, separated the Allied forces from their next objective: mainland Italy.

THE INVASION OF ITALY

At dawn on 3 September, British and Canadian forces crossed the Straits of Messina and landed unopposed at Reggio di Calabria. Other landings followed, and the naval base at Taranto was easily secured. The Italians signed an armistice with the Allies on 8 September 1943, their fleet sailed to Malta to surrender.

In response, a furious Hitler occupied Italy with 16 German divisions, commanded by *Generalfeldmarschall* Kesselring. Hitler perceived the entire population of Italy as guilty of treachery, and intended to make an example of them. His forces immediately disarmed over half a million Italian soldiers, sending many to forced labour camps. German paratroopers seized control of Rome, and the SS began the systematic rounding up of what was left of the city's Jewish population.

OPERATION *AVALANCHE* – SALERNO

The Gulf of Salerno, the most obvious site for further landings, was quickly defended by the 16th Panzer Division, reformed after the original unit's destruction at Stalingrad the previous year. They greeted the Allied invaders who arrived on 8 September with a potent show of force. The US VI Corp and their British allies were pinned down on the beaches and nearby fields and orchards by intense German artillery fire from higher ground – the operation, codenamed *Avalanche*, had stalled before it had even properly begun.

The only significant Allied advance was by Lieutenant Colonel William Darby's Rangers, who seized areas along the Chiunzi Pass, overlooking the mountain road to Naples. This allowed them to call down bombardments from the warships in the gulf to wreak havoc on the German supplies and reinforcements coming down the road.

The Allies needed every small advantage they could get. The Hermann Göring Panzer Division and the 15th and 16th Panzergrenadier Divisions had quickly reinforced the German lines. An attack by the 36th Division of Texas National Guardsmen on 13 September to capture the hilltop village of Altavilla was bloodily repulsed, and a subsequent German offensive almost forced the US force to re-embark and abandon the invasion. The British 8th Army, advancing north from Calabria on Italy's eastern coast, was held up by the narrow, winding highland roads and the numerous bridges that had been destroyed by the Germans before they had withdrawn from the southern peninsula. There was no hope of them coming to the aid of the beleagured Americans any time soon.

Fresh hope came from the battleships HMS *Warspite* and HMS *Valiant*, which had arrived from Malta, providing much needed fire support from the sea. By 15 September, the Americans had also stopped the German Panzer breakthrough, firing their 105mm guns at virtually point-blank range with their backs to the sea. The 82nd Airborne Division was also dropped to reinforce the invaders. Gradually, the German tanks and artillery were thinned by concentrated bombardment from the heavy guns of the US Navy and Royal Navy, and by continuous air attacks from Allied bombers. The Americans developed a new bombing tactic called 'Putting the city in the street', where a town was reduced to rubble making it impossible for enemy transport and supply vehicles to use the blocked roads. In this case, the town of Battipaglia, just behind the German lines, was smashed to ruin by bombing raids, cutting off the Germans from their supply route. Italian civilians suffered terribly in this campaign, caught between the fury of the occupying German soldiers, wreaking revenge for their 'treacherous' surrender, and the hard-nosed military pragmatism of the Allied forces.

The German withdrawal from Salerno began on 18 September. Kesselring pulled his army back to the River Volturno north of Naples. The overwhelming superiority of firepower from the Allied navies and air forces had proved irresistible. In response, the British on the left of the US beachhead attacked north to secure the Sorrento Peninsula, from which they could begin marching on Naples. By 25 September, the 8th Army finally reached the US 5th Army, and the southern 'foot' of Italy was firmly under Allied control. From there, Allied bombers could launch raids on southern Germany, Austria and the Ploesti oilfields. Naples, despoiled by the retreating Germans, was taken without contest on 25 September. Hitler's grip on mainland Europe was slowly slipping.

THE GUSTAV LINE

The Fuhrer had one consolation – German spies had learned that Mussolini was imprisoned at Gran Sasso, a ski resort in the Appenines north of Rome. On 12 September, a team of *Waffen-SS* special forces led by one of Hitler's favourite commanders, *SS-Hauptsturmfuhrer* Otto Skorzeny, and *Fallschirmjager*, landed there in gliders and rescued Hitler's ally. Mussolini was subsequently installed as the leader of a

puppet state in the North of Italy – the *Republica Sociale Italiana*, with headquarters in Salò on Lake Garda – mostly to give the German occupation the semblance of legitimacy.

Hitler was desperate to cling on to the resources and industries of northern Italy, and was aware that if the whole of Italy would fall, this might undermine the morale of his Balkan allies, threaten the German stranglehold on southern France and Greece and even potentially attract neutral Turkey into the war on the Allied side. He had vacillated between the advice of Kesselring, who had urged him to reinforce southern Italy before the Allies could gain a foothold there, and Rommel, who argued that the best use of German forces in the region was to abandon the south and concentrate on defending the north. Hitler was at first swayed by Rommel, hence the relative ease with which the Allies gained a foothold on the southern tip of Italy. Only after the Italian armistice, and the setbacks suffered by the Allies at Salerno – an alleged display of the weakness of their armies – did Hitler firmly resolve to back Kesselring. The Germans bolstered their defences along the foreboding highland ridges south of Rome. The invading Allies would pay a dear toll for their advance into the Italian heartlands, but the

The fight for the tobacco factory, VI Corps sector, by Steve Noon © Osprey Publishing Ltd. Taken from Campaign 257: Salerno 1943.

LEGENDS OF GERMANY
OTTO SKORZENY

Otto Skorzeny began his career as a commissioned officer in the Waffen-SS and saw action in Holland, France, the Balkans and the Eastern Front, where he was wounded. During his recuperation period, he intensively studied unconventional warfare methods and became a vociferous supporter of special force actions behind enemy lines. He was put in charge of training and developing such units, which he also personally led in several operations on all fronts, earning many decorations like the Knight's Cross of the Iron Cross with Oak Leaves. The most famous of his exploits are arguably the airborne liberation of deposed fascist dictator Benito Mussolini from his mountain prison, and the special English-speaking units that were deployed in US uniform during the Battle of the Bulge. After the war, he remained in character by escaping from the military prison that was holding him and working with Nazi underground movements for years, finally switching to a more 'normal' career training international mercenaries until the 1970s, when he died of cancer at age 67.

Cost: 195pts (Veteran)
Team: 1 officer and up to 2 other men
Weapons: Submachine gun, pistol or rifle/carbine as depicted on the model
Options:
- Skorzeny may be accompanied by up to 2 men at a cost of +13pts per man

Special Rules:
- The most dangerous man in Europe: Skorzeny's Morale bonus is +4 and the range of his ability is 12"
- Long Jumper: if Skorzeny is in your force, half of your Brandenburgers (or any other German special forces units), rounding up, can deploy by 'Long Jump' unconventional techniques. These units are left in Reserve and must Outflank. However, when they become available, they can enter the battlefield from either the declared short edge or any point along the enemy's table edge.

37 German divisions that were tied up defending the region were drawn from the Eastern Front, where they were badly needed, and from Western Europe, which would soon see a new front opened following the Normandy landings.

North of Naples, the Allies soon ran into German holding positions along the River Volturno. On 13 October, an artillery barrage supported the British and US troops fording the river, and a crossing point was secured the following day. By now, the autumn rains had set in, turning the terrain into deep mud and sapping the morale of the Allied soldiers. Bridge after bridge over raging rivers had been destroyed by the retreating enemy, and narrow mountain roads were heavily mined. The Allies' progress was painfully slow. Leading tanks were taken out by anti-tank guns hidden along the routes to further delay the advance. Hilltop villages had to be methodically cleared of enemy units by the infantry, causing further misery and delay.

Kesselring made his stand 30km north of the Volturno, along the Gustav Line, which stretched 140km from the Adriatic in the west to the Tyrrhenian Sea on the east. Three great obstacles guarded the route to Rome: the Mignano Gap flanked by forbidding mountains, the raging Rapido River, and the seemingly impregnable peak of Monte Cassino.

At this point, seven American divisions were withdrawn to the UK to prepare them for the Normandy landings planned for the following summer. The Allies were now not strong enough to break quickly through the German defences they faced. Instead, what followed was a long winter of bitter fighting. In this mountainous terrain, the infantry came to the fore, and the Allies' massive advantage in tanks was negated. Positioned on the higher slopes, the dug-in German defenders had the clear advantage.

On 5 November, an attempt was made by the 201st Guards Brigade of the British X Corps, on the western end of the Gustav Line, to seize Monte Camino in order to outflank the Mignano Gap. The bare rock provided little shelter either from the incessant freezing rain or from the mortar fire of the 15th Panzergrenadier Division defending the higher slopes. After a hellish few days, the British were forced to withdraw. Another attack on Murder Mountain, as it came to be known, was unleashed on 2 December. Almost a thousand American artillery pieces let loose on the defenders, while the British climbed the rocky slopes as torrential rain poured down. The mountain was taken after several days of hard fighting. The Americans attempted a parallel assault against enemy defences on Monte La Difensa. The 1st Special Service Force, accompanying the US troops, took the summit the following dawn and repulsed the ferocious German counter-attacks against them.

With these objectives taken, the Germans defending the road through the Mignano Gap could now be outflanked, and the Americans attacked the fortified village of San Pietro, and the artillery positions at Monte Lungo. Both these positions were taken after several days with heavy Allied losses. Fighting alongside the Americans was a brigade of Italian Alpini, cut to pieces as they stormed the machine-guns of their former, now hated, allies. Exhausted, dishevelled, perpetually soaked from rain, the troops of the 5th Army and British X Corps soldiered on, as the Germans withdrew to their next line of defence.

Across the Appenines, on the Adriatic side of operations, the advance of Montgomery's 8th Army was delayed by the heavy rains, which bogged down his tanks and rendered air support impossible. The River Sangro proved an almost insurmountable obstacle, its swollen waters sweeping away the pontoon bridges erected across it. It was not until 27 November that the 2nd New Zealand Division got a foothold on the opposite bank,

An Italian villa plays host to the deadly 88...

allowing the British to whittle away at the Germans defending the high ground on the opposite side of the Sangro valley. But the advance was slow, exacerbated by a devastating *Luftwaffe* raid on the port of Bari which delayed the provision of much-needed supplied to the troops further north.

As winter set in, Montgomery ordered the Canadian 1st Division to attack the coastal town of Ortona. The Canadians advanced well until halted at a mine-strewn ravine south-west of Ortona, where the 90th Panzergrenadier Division and 1st *Fallschirmjäger* paratroop division held the line for nine days against wave after wave of enemy assaults, causing over 2,000 Canadian casualties. Even when the line was broken on 21 December, the German paratroopers held the ruins of Ortona for a further week, stalling the Allied advance until the end of the December.

With their advance going far slower than expected, the Allies attempted to break the impasse with an amphibious landing close to Rome, to draw away the enemy from the Gustav Line. The site of the landings was decided to be the beaches at Anzio along the Tyrrhenian coast, 100km behind the German lines. To give the Anzio landings a chance of success, on 19 January, General Mark Clark's 5th Army launched an all-out attack to cross the River Rapido, the

second of the three major obstacles blocking the route to Rome. The Americans would attack on the centre, with the British X Corps advancing close to the sea on the left, and new reinforcements in the form of a French Expeditionary Corps with two divisions of North African *goumier* mountain fighters supporting the right.

A British night attack across the River Garigliano, formed at the confluence of the Rapido and Liri rivers, was repulsed by the Germans who scattered the British assault boats by opening sluice-gates upstream, causing the river to turn into a torrent. The next night, the American 36th Division attempted to cross the Gari, but many units became lost in the thick mist, blundered into mine fields left by the Germans, or fell prey to enemy machine-guns as they crossed. Those few who managed to cross were recalled. Another attempt was ordered the following day, but withdrew after intense shelling and mortaring. The division suffered two thousand casualties with none of the objectives achieved. However, Kesselring, alarmed by these attacks, moved the 29th and 90th Panzergrenadier Divisions out of reserve to reinforce his troops defending the Rapido and Garilgliano rivers. This meant that Anzio was now unprotected.

ANZIO AND MONTE CASSINO

The landings at Anzio took the Germans by complete surprise. The US 3rd Division and the British 1st Infantry Division, supported by Commandos and three battalions of Rangers, secured the undefended beach on 22 January 1944. But the commander of this force, Major General J.P. Lucas, concentrated on merely securing the beachhead and the surrounding plain, and did not advance from this position until two days later. By that time, the hills surrounding the plain was bristling with Germans hurriedly brought down from northern Italy by a panicked Kesselring. From their advantageous positions, German artillery rained death on the invaders below. On 23 January, the US 3rd Division and the Rangers attacked, but were driven back by a vastly superior enemy force, with the Rangers almost eliminated as a fighting force. The overcast skies made Allied air support extremely difficult, and by now the 60,000 strong Allied force faced German reinforcements almost twice their number. German patrols whittled away at the perimeter of the beachhead, and the roar of German heavy guns thundered day and night.

While the Allies at Anzio braced themselves for the inevitable German counter-attack, the stalemate along the banks of the Rapido continued, with the infantry, freezing in the grip of winter, sheltering from the artillery duel wailing overhead. However, by the end of January, the Allies made a few small gains. The French corps in the north-east crossed the River Secco and penetrated the Gustav Line to capture Monte Belvedere, fighting from ridge to ridge in mid-winter, they suffered over 8,000 casualties, but refused to cede ground. On 30 January, the US 34th Division forded the Rapido north of Cassino and in the ensuing days fought its way to the rear of Monte Cassino. Having secured its position, the badly mauled division had to be replaced by the 4th Indian Division, and Lieutenant General Bernard Freyberg, commander of the New Zealand corps, now took command of the attack on Monte Cassino.

At Anzio, on 4 February, the Germans attacked the British salient, driving flocks of sheep ahead of them to clear the

Fighting for 'The Factory', 11 February 1944, by Peter Dennis © Osprey Publishing Ltd. Taken from Campaign 155: Anzio 1944.

minefields laid by the Allies. The British 1st Infantry Division lost 1,500 men, and fell back before the irresistible surge of German infantry and Panzers. Another German attack took place on 7 February, and was only held off by the Allied artillery and the firepower of the Allied warships anchored offshore. The Germans tried again on 16 February, with the 3rd Panzergrenadier Division and 26th Panzer Division embroiled against the US 45th Division and the British 56th Division at the town of Aprilia. Overeager to present Hitler with the decisive victory he demanded at Anzio, the German commander Mackensen simply sent wave after wave of troops and armour against his enemies, hoping that sheer numbers would drive them back into the sea, but he hadn't accounted for the ferocity of the Allies massed artillery, which blew his formations to pieces. His unsophisticated tactics cost him over 5,000 men, and the Allied held on with grim determination. German reinforcements thrown in on 18 February merely added to Mackensen's long list of casualties.

While the Germans threw men at the Allied salients at Anzio, the Allies fixed their sights on Monte Cassino. Freyberg was convinced that the ancient monastery on the mountain's peak was harbouring German defenders and artillery spotters, and managed to persuade his superior, General Alexander, that he was right, against the advice of many other senior Allied officers. On 15 February, the monastery was reduced to rubble by waves of Allied bombers. Freyberg had been wrong, the Germans had respected the wishes of the Abbot and avoided deploying troops within the monastery. The several

The American advance stalls as the Italians stand their ground.

hundred civilians sheltering within the monastery were killed. It was a significant propaganda coup for the Nazis, and by turning the monastery into a military target, the Allies simply gave the Germans an excuse to occupy the ruins, strengthening their defences on the mountain.

The 2nd New Zealand Division and 4th Indian Division were now mobilised against the town of Cassino, which was defended by the 1st *Fallschirmjäger* Division. The rain bogged down the attack, the poor visibility grounding the Allied aircraft and the waterlogged terrain ensuring that Freyberg could not use his tanks. For the rest of the month, the battle for Monte Cassino remained a static war of attrition.

Back at Anzio, Mackensen attacked the allies hunkered down along the beachhead once more on 29 February, but still could not shift them, the assault once again halted by the Allied artillery barrage. The Germans here were running low on artillery ammunition while day by day the Allies were shipping in more and more troops and weaponry. As winter slowly receded, the Allied forces gradually increased the number of men within the beachhead to 100,000, but the battle remained in the balance – the Germans couldn't shift the Allies, but the Allies couldn't break out.

The rain finally stopped on 15 March. The US 15th Air Force seized the opportunity to make a heavy raid on Cassino, though some of their bombs fell on the Allied lines too. Allied artillery raked the town as well, in preparation for an assault by

Freyberg's forces. For over a week, the New Zealanders and the Indians tried to shift the German paratroopers defending the ruined town. The Allies' tanks were hampered by the rubble-strewn streets, and the German paratroopers fought with fanatical determination. After over a week of fighting, Freyberg withdrew his forces with heavy losses.

With the arrival of spring, General Alexander planned a fresh offensive against the Gustav Line. Codenamed Operation *Diadem*, 500,000 Allied soldiers would assault the German defences, swamping them with sheer weight of numbers. Elaborate deceptions were used, such as building fake bunkers where the attacks would be launched from to give the enemy the impression that the Allies were going on the defensive. False radio reports and dummy landing craft insinuated that another amphibious landing was being planned.

It was not until May that the preparations for this assault were ready. On 11 May, artillery opened up all across the Allied lines, pounding the German defences. At Cassino, the II Polish Corps, led by General Wladyslaw Anders, which had replaced Freyberg's demoralised forces, charged the enemy lines, but were cut to ribbons as they faced a German force twice the expected strength. The 8th Indian Division, attacking across the Rapido against the fortified village of Sant'Angelo, were also badly mauled, until engineers secured bridges across the river and the Gurkhas, supported by tanks, took the

A monstrous Elefant bars the way.

village in a ferocious charge. The Garigliano River again proved a difficult obstacle, this time for the US II Corps, and the French divisions, positioned between the British and Americans, were also bloodily repulsed. However, their commander, General Juin, diverted his men to attack the German strongpoint on Monte Majo. Supported by a heavy artillery barrage, his hard-bitten *goumiers*, expert mountain-fighters, cleared the peak of enemy defenders. Suffering 2,000 casualties, the French had broken the Gustav Line.

Despite their losses, the steadfast courage of the Poles prevailed at Cassino, and they gradually encircled the enemy, forcing the paratroopers to withdraw. Monte Cassino fell to the Poles on May 18th, but at a cost of 4,000 men. Kesselring drew his forces back to the Hitler Line, about twenty kilometres behind the fractured Gustav Line, but his men were harried all the way there by the French. The 8th Army, now commanded by Lieutenant General Sir Oliver Leese (Montgomery had returned to Britain to help oversee the Normandy landings), finally broke the defenders at the Liri Valley, and together with Mark Clark's Americans, marched on the Hitler Line.

THE FALL OF ROME

Kesselring could only hold this last line of defence before Rome by moving troops there from the force besieging the beachhead at Anzio. On 23 May, the divisions at Anzio, freshly reinforced and now stronger than the German force surrounding them, pushed forward and, despite heavy casualties, forced the enemy to withdraw. The US II Corps on the coast, finding that their opponents were in retreat, linked up with the Anzio beachhead. The Hitler Line did not hold for long. The Germans were in general retreat to the north of the country, and by 4 June, Rome fell to the Allies without a fight.

General Mark Clark was jubilant that he was the first to enter Rome, beating the British to that honour, but in doing so he had deliberately ignored a direct order from his superior officer, General Alexander, to divert from Rome and cut off Kesselring's retreat. Had he done this, there was a good chance that the main body of German troops in Italy would have been surrounded and eventually forced to surrender. As it was, Clark had his glory, and the German army in Italy escaped north to fight on.

Clark's liberation of Rome soon lost the limelight to the Normandy Landings later that month. To accompany the invasion of northern France, the equivalent of seven divisions of American and French troops were redeployed from Italy to participate in Operation *Dragoon*, an invasion of the south of France. Clark received replacements in the form of the Brazilian 1st Infantry Division.

THE GOTHIC LINE

With a reduced force, during the summer of 1944, the Allies advanced north of Rome, liberating Florence before being blocked by the Gothic Line, Germany's last major line of defence in Italy. Stretching coast to coast from just north of Pisa in the west to just south of Rimini in the east, it crossed the peaks of the Appenine ridge between Florence and Bologna.

Control of a port in northern Italy was vital for the Allies' success, and on 18 July, after a month-long battle, the Polish II Corps captured Ancona on the Adriatic coast. This allowed the commencement of Operation *Olive* in late August 1944, when the US 5th Army and British 8th Army both penetrated the Gothic Line on separate fronts, but without a decisive breakthrough. In the autumn, an attempt was made to capture Bologna from the Germans, but the Allies narrowly failed in this objective after fierce fighting.

The Allied advance through Italy was stalled. Mark Clark took over the role of commander of Allied ground troops in Italy from General Alexander in December 1945, and he was forced to adopt a strategy of 'offensive defence', whittling down the strength and morale of the Germans holding the line with incessant raids, while ensuring that no German counter-attack could push through the Allied battlefront. The harsh Italian winter of 1944–45 denied the Allies their advantage in armour and air superiority. Moreover, a significant number of British and Commonwealth troops from the 8th Army were transferred to participate in the liberation of Greece, and to reinforce the Allied gains in north-west Europe. The Germans experienced their share of the suffering meted out by the cruel winter, and also had other problems behind the Gothic Line, as Italian partisans waged a bitter war against the occupiers.

With the thaw in late February/early March 1945, the Allies were now able to strike. Operation *Encore* witnessed the eviction of German troops from key positions in the Appennine mountains, at Monte Castello, Monte Belvedere and Castelnuovo. Units from US IV Corps (the Brazilian Expeditionary Force and the US 10th Mountain Division) secured these positions after some hard fighting in treacherous mountainous conditions.

The Allied guns thundered across the Gothic Line on 9 April, accompanied by the scream of Allied aircraft, strafing and bombing enemy positions. The Allies' assaults bore fruit, as by 18 April the 8th Army broke through the eastern enemy lines at the Argenta Gap, allowing them to use their tanks to encircle the defenders of Bologna, who were pressed by the US IV Corps advancing from the Apennines. Bologna fell to the Allies on 21

April, and those Allied forces that had bypassed the city reached the River Po on the following days. Beyond the Po, lay the last Italian cities in German hands – Venice, Trieste, Milan and Turin. Beyond the northern Italian border was Austria. Retreating on all fronts, and facing a general insurrection from the Italian partisans, the remnants of the Axis forces in Italy surrendered on 29 April – nine days later, Germany also surrendered unconditionally, and Victory in Europe was declared.

The Germans had resisted in Italy almost until the very end of the war in Europe. Churchill had been very much mistaken when he referred to Italy as the 'soft underbelly'. Overall Allied casualties for the campaign totalled over 320,000 and the Axis suffered slightly more – these were much higher figures than any of the other campaigns fought around the Mediterranean.

Churchill's plans to use Italy as a springboard to launch an Allied attack on the Balkans came to nothing, and the Balkan region came firmly under the control of the Soviets during the partition of Europe following the war. However, the Allies' efforts in Italy tied up Axis troops and armaments that could have been used to stem the tide of the Soviet advance into Germany, and to bolster the defenders of Nazi-occupied Western Europe. The Allied campaign in Italy was hard-won and achieved at a great cost in shattered lives, but it undoubtedly played its part in the destruction of the Nazi regime.

A BAR team from the 92nd 'Buffalo' Division duels with a German sniper, by Johnny Shumate © Osprey Publishing Ltd. Taken from Weapon 15: The Browning Automatic Rifle.

FIGHTING THE INVASION OF ITALY USING *BOLT ACTION*

In Sicily and Italy, the protagonists leave behind the dusty, desert conditions of North Africa and fight their battles in a more temperate climate. Gone also are the wide expanses of uninhabited sandy wilderness, ideal for sweeping manoeuvres by highly mobile military forces. Instead, the Allies face hilly, often mountainous, terrain, where fortified hilltop villages have to be taken one by one, rapid rivers have to be crossed under enemy fire, and narrow mountain roads severely restrict the movement of advancing armour and other vehicles. Significantly, the US Army no longer comprises of green recruits, but of tough, experienced soldiers who have learned much since their baptism of fire in Tunisia. But their German adversaries refuse to give ground without a bitter fight, and despite being on the back foot, intend to turn Italy into an inferno for the invaders.

THEATRE SELECTORS

The following theatre selectors should be used to represent the forces involved in Sicily and the invasion of Italy:

GERMANS
• Defence of Italy Reinforced Platoon (*Armies of Germany*, page 85).

ITALIANS
• Defence of Sicily Reinforced Platoon (*Armies of Italy and the Axis*, page 35).

USA
• Operation *Husky* Reinforced Platoon (*Armies of the United States*, page 60)
• Operation *Avalanche* Reinforced Platoon (*Armies of the United States*, page 63)
• Cassino Reinforced Platoon (*Armies of the United States*, page 64)
• Anzio, the Road to Rome Reinforced Platoon (*Armies of the United States*, page 65)

BRITISH & COMMONWEALTH
• Monte Cassino Reinforced Platoon (*Armies of Great Britain*, page 72)
• Indian Division Reinforced Platoon (page 23).

FREE FRENCH
• Free French Reinforced Platoon (page 19).

ITALY INVADED SPECIAL RULES

The following special rules are pertinent to battles fought in this campaign:

MULTINATIONAL FORCES

Feel free to use these rules for mixed Allied forces. A German force can field some Italian units from the Defence of Sicily Reinforced Platoon to represent Italian troops still fighting for the fascist cause, such as the San Marco Marine Division and the Monterosa Mountain Division of Army Group Liguria at the Gothic Line. Note that later in this chapter you'll find rules for fielding Allied Italian units, though these count as an Infantry Section in an Allied army rather than a separate reinforced platoon. The rules are on page 120.

DUG-IN

You can use these rules for any battle fought in Sicily or Italy. See page 124 for the rules.

CONTROL OF THE SKIES

The Allies have control of the skies throughout the Italian campaign – see page 125. This is fine for the summer months. However, for any game set during either of the two bitter Italian winters suffered by the combatants, both sides count as having reduced airpower to represent the low cloud, driving rain, fog and other wintry conditions that can hinder flight.

GERONIMO!

The airdrops during the invasion of Sicily, and the drop of the 82nd Airborne at Salerno, can be recreated using the rules on page 126. For added drama, an American player using the airdrop to deploy units should roll a D6 before the battle starts – on a 4+, he rolls on the Preparatory Bombardment chart (*Bolt Action* page 118) for each of his own units that is to be parachuted in, representing his trigger-happy anti-aircraft gunners mistaking their side's planes for enemy aircraft. Any pin markers suffered affect the units as soon as they land. Any hits suffered take place immediately.

GLIDERS

Gliders were used to insert some units into Sicily, and the rules for using these can be found on page 127.

NIGHT FIGHTING

Many raids and some larger actions in Sicily and Italy took place at night, or at dawn or dusk. The rules for night fighting are on page 129.

MINEFIELDS

The Germans used minefields prolifically in their defence of Sicily and Italy. The Allies too used mines when they had to go on the defensive. See page 131 for rules on using minefields.

LIMITED FUEL SUPPLY

Fuel was certainly not an issue for the Allies at this stage, thanks to the Americans' prodigious supply chain. The problems with fuel supplies that the Axis forces experienced in North Africa were alleviated due to their closer proximity to their supply centres, but the constant bombing of roads and railways in Axis-held Italy still made things difficult for them, and towards the end of the war, with most of Germany reduced to rubble, and the loss of the Ploesti oilfields to the Soviets in August 1944, the German forces in Italy felt the pinch.

The Limited Fuel Supply rules (page 133) affects all Axis units fighting battles set during the Autumn of 1944 onwards (for example, Axis units defending the Gothic Line).

USING CAPTURED ENEMY VEHICLES

The Allies, with access to plentiful war materiel thanks to the limitless pockets of the Americans, would have no use for captured enemy vehicles. However, the Axis side might be more desperate, so if both players agree the Axis player can use this rule (detailed on page 133). Both sides could use Italian vehicles in their armies, see the Armies of Italy and the Axis book.

AMPHIBIOUS ASSAULTS

Use these rules when playing the Blood on the Beaches scenario to represent the opposed landings at Salerno (see page 134).

MUD

Almost as bad as the constant, withering shellfire and gunfire of the enemy that the Allies experienced while stalled at the Gustav Line was the sea of mud, caused by the incessant freezing rain. For any games set in the Gustav Line during the winter months of 1943–44, use the rules on page 136 to represent the misery this caused the troops.

SNOW ON THE GOTHIC LINE

No major actions were fought at the Gothic Line during the winter of 1944–45, as snow and ice froze hostilities. However, if you want to play out one of the many raids that took place between the combatants during this time, treat the entire tabletop as rough ground, except to units equipped with skis, to represent the freezing, wintry conditions.

Commonwealth troops cautiously advance into the unknown

SCENARIOS

GENERAL SCENARIOS

All the scenarios from the *Bolt Action* rulebook are suitable for battles set during the invasion of Sicily and the Italian campaign:

- Scenario 1: Envelopment (page 108)
- Scenario 2: Maximum Attrition (page 110)
- Scenario 3: Point Defence (page 112)
- Scenario 4: Hold Until Relieved (page 114)
- Scenario 5: Top Secret (page 115)
- Scenario 6: Demolition (page 116)

Some of the special scenarios detailed earlier in this book can be adapted for use during the invasion of Sicily and the Italian campaign, as follows:

- Blood on the Beaches (page 75). This scenario is ideal to represent the opposed beach landing at Salerno – note that the beach in this scenario will be heavily fortified, as described in the scenario rules. The US forces had a quiet landing, but the two British divisions had to fight their way onshore, as did the 36th Texas Division at Paestum, 38km south of Salerno. Note that the Allied seaborne landings at Sicily and across the Straits of Messina, as well as at Anzio, took the Germans by surprise and were unopposed.
- The Delaying Action scenario (page 29) can be adapted with the Germans as the defenders, to represent one of the many actions fought by the Axis forces to cover the withdrawal of their main army as the Allies advance through Sicily and Italy.
- The Control the Heights scenario (page 82) can be used to play out one of the many actions in the hills of Sicily, or the highlands of Italy where an Allied force had to wrest control of high ground from the German defenders.

In addition, there are six scenarios detailed in this chapter, which allow you to play out battles representing various actions specifically pertinent to those experienced by the troops in Italy. These are:

- Bridgehead (page 102)
- Assault on Altavilla (page 104)
- The River Runs Red – Crossing the Rapido (page 107)
- Backs to the Sea – Anzio (page 109)
- Monte Cassino – Attempt on Monastery Hill (page 111)
- The Gothic Line – War of Attrition (page 114)

TERRAIN

The terrain, of course, varies depending on the battlefield, but unlike battles in the desert, there should be lots of good cover, obstacles, buildings and so on.

We can roughly split the general geography of the Sicilian and Italian battle sites into five types:

BEACHES

As at Salerno and Anzio. One third of the table (the Allied half) might be featureless sand, with dunes marking the edge of the coastline, and verdant, sometimes steep, hills rising inland, dotted with woods. You might have a few seaside buildings along the coast, or in a more remote sector of the beach, low cliffs jutting into the sand.

UPLANDS

This represents the Sicilian hills, or the foothills of the Apennines in mainland Italy. Use as many hills as possible on the table. In Sicily and southern Italy, the ground would be dry scrubland, with little tree cover, other than cultivated olive groves or the suchlike. Further north, the land is lusher and wooded. Although underpopulated, there might be a hillside farm or an ancient medieval village, or even a villa or castle with a road leading past it. A river might flow from the hills, with an ancient, and strategically important, bridge.

HIGHLANDS

You'll need lots of big hills to represent Italy's mountainous region. The Apennines run along the entire length of mainland Italy, and were vital to the German defence, with the Gustav Line in the south and the Gothic Line in the north crossing them. The terrain will be rocky, steep and treacherous. Perhaps a narrow road might wind alongside the mountains, and, if you're an intrepid modeller, you could make a gorge to bisect the table. A mountain river can prove a challenging obstacle to an invading force. A small settlement might hug a mountainside, or the area could be completely uninhabited.

LOWLANDS

These include the fertile areas just inland from the coast, and expansive river valleys – highly populated, dotted with farms and farmland, and traversed by a road. Perhaps the edge of a village or town flanks one edge of the table? Most of the table is flat, with field boundaries and woodland providing cover, and perhaps a wide river providing a defensible line for the Germans.

URBAN

If you have enough Mediterranean style buildings, you could stage a city fight, such as the assault on Bologna in the latter stages of the campaign. Because this was not as common a feature of the war in Italy as in other theatres, we won't reproduce the rules for urban combat here, but direct you to the *Ostfront Bolt Action* supplement, which has them on page 118.

SCENARIO 12: BRIDGEHEAD

One of the first objectives following the landings at Sicily was to secure communication routes that would allow a swift deployment of forces to attack inland. One of these was Ponte Grande, a bridge over the River Anape just south of Syracuse. A platoon of British soldiers from the South Staffordshire Regiment had successfully landed their Horsa glider on target nearby and captured the bridge in a dawn assault, attacking it from both sides and forcing the Italian 120th Coastal Infantry Regiment to abandon their pillboxes on the north bank. The Staffords defused the charges laid by the Italians, ensuring the bridge's safety.

The gunfire attracted British reinforcements, though by 06:30 only 87 men defended the bridge. Their mission was to hold it until joined by the British 5th Infantry Division marching from the beaches at Cassibile 11km to the south. These were expected at 10:00,

Ponte Grande immediately became a magnet for Italian soldiers of the 206 Coastal Division, mobilizing in response to the Allied landings. The Staffords fought off a series of counter-attacks, while the deadline for their reinforcements ticked by. By midday, the British faced the combined might of the Italian 385th Coastal Battalion and the 1st Battalion, 75th (Napoli) Infantry Regiment, who attacked the bridge from both sides. For over three hours the defenders of the bridge held out, until there were only fifteen left alive and unwounded. They carried on the fight until their ammunition ran out. A few escaped, but most where made prisoners-of-war. The Italians began to set up their demolition fuses on the bridge once more.

A mere 45 minutes later, a unit of Royal Scots Fusiliers from the 5th Infantry Division arrived – the first of the heavily delayed British reinforcements. These retook the bridge before the Italians could destroy it, and secured the road to Syracuse.

The following scenario is designed to recreate the intense battle fought over the Ponte Grande, though you can adapt it for use in any World War II theatre where one side is attempting to wrest control of a bridge from the other.

FORCES

This scenario is designed to be played with equal points values on both sides. The following reinforced platoons should be used to represent the forces involved:

LEGENDS OF BRITAIN & THE COMMONWEALTH

MAD JACK CHURCHILL

"Any officer who goes into action without his sword is improperly dressed." – J. Churchill.

Born in Surrey in 1906, Jack Churchill was a many-talented man – amongst other things, he excelled at archery (he represented Britain at the 1939 World Archery championships) and bagpipe-playing. In his early life he served in the army in Burma, and then worked as a newspaper editor, an actor and a male model. At the outbreak of the war he joined the army again. As part of the BEF, he went into battle in France carrying a Scottish broadsword at his side and a longbow and arrow on his back. In May 1940 he become the only British soldier to have killed an enemy in World War II with a bow, when he shot dead a German NCO.

After Dunkirk, he joined the Commandos, with whom he participated in many actions in almost every single theatre where British troops fought, earning many decorations. He used to go into battle not only with broadsword and bow, but also with bagpipes. In 1943, in Sicily, he led a single corporal against a German observation and mortar position behind enemy lines, capturing 42 prisoners... he himself was eventually captured and held in Germany until the end of the war in Europe. Shipped with all hurry to Burma to fight the Japanese, he arrived too late – the war was over. Disappointed, he allegedly commented: "If it wasn't for those damn Yanks, we could have kept the war going another 10 years!"

Cost: 195pts (Veteran)

Team: 1 officer and up to 2 other men

Weapons: Jack Churchill is equipped with broadsword and bow (counts as a rifle). Other men are equipped with submachine gun, pistol or rifle/carbine as depicted on the model.

Options:
• Jack Churchill may be accompanied by up to 2 men at a cost of +14pts per man.

Special Rules:
• Lead by example (and bagpiping!): Churchill's Morale bonus is +4. Whenever his order die shows down or rally, Churchill is playing his bagpipes, and so the range of his Morale bonus is increased to 24".
• Tough fighters
• Behind enemy lines: When Outflanking as described on page 119 of the *Bolt Action* rulebook, this unit ignores the –1 modifier to the Order test for coming onto the table.

ITALIANS
• Defence of Sicily Reinforced Platoon (*Armies of Italy and the Axis*, page 35)

BRITISH
• Glider Landing Platoon Selector (page 127)
• Monte Cassino Reinforced Platoon (*Armies of Great Britain*, page 72)

The British player should field two separate forces of equal points value (each equal to half the points value of the enemy army). The first force should be created using the Glider Landing Platoon Selector. The second, the Monte Cassino Reinforced Platoon.

Note – if you want to keep things historical, no armoured vehicle can be fielded by either player in this game.

SET-UP

TERRAIN
This scenario is played across the long edge of the table. The bridge runs right down the centre and is 12" wide (6" "either side of the middle line). On the Italian (Northern) table edge there is 12" of riverbank. The river on either side of the bridge is deep water (see Movement in Water, page 134).

DEPLOYMENT
The Italian defender deploys up to half his force on the riverbank, within 12" of his table edge. These units may begin the game hidden. This area should be fortified with obstacles and up to three pillboxes. Any units not set up at the beginning of the game are held back in reserve.

The British attacker sets up at least half his force on the bridge, within 12" of his own (southern) table edge (this will be his entire Glider Landing Platoon). If you want to give the British player an added challenge, his platoon should be deployed using the Glider Landing rules on page 128. The entire platoon counts as being in a single glider.

Any units not set up at the beginning of the game are held back in reserve.

SPECIAL RULES

FIRST TURN
The battle begins.

DEMOLITION CHARGES
The Italian player places five counters at various points on the bridge. These represent potential demolition charges that must be neutralised by the British player. The counters may be placed anywhere, as long as they are no closer than 6" from another counter.

To defuse a demolition charge, a British infantry unit must be issued a *down* order while one or more of its members are in base contact with the counter. They must always roll an order test to issue this *down* order (even if they are not pinned), as defusing a bomb whilst under fire is a difficult task at best. If they succeed, remove the counter. If they fail the test, the counter stays but the unit still gets the *down* order.

DELAYED REINFORCEMENTS
The British 5th Infantry was severely delayed in getting to the bridge. To represent this, the British player cannot begin to bring on reserves until Turn 4 of the game.

HOLD AT ALL COSTS
The Staffords are utterly dedicated to fulfilling their orders to the last man (or the last round of bullets). Any unit from the Glider Landing Platoon have the Fanatics special rule until Turn 6, when their ammo begins to run out.

DUG-IN
The defenders can dig in. See page 124.

CONTROL OF THE SKIES
The Allies have control of the skies – see page 125.

OBJECTIVE
The British player must diffuse all demolition charges, while the Italian player is trying to stop them.

GAME DURATION
Keep a count of how many turns have elapsed as the game is played. At the end of Turn 6, roll a die. On a result of 1, 2 or 3 the game ends, on a roll of 4, 5 or 6 play one further turn.

VICTORY!
At the end of the game all charges that have not yet been defused are triggered. The Italian player rolls a die for each charge still active – on a 4+ it explodes, but on a 3 or less it's a dud. If two or more of the charges explode, the bridge is destroyed and the Italians win the game, otherwise the British win the game.

SCENARIO 13: ASSAULT ON ALTAVILLA

Having landed at Paestum on 9 September 1943, in support of the Salerno landings to the north, the 36th Texas Infantry Division had to fight their way up a beach that had been heavily fortified by the defending Germans. After successfully forging a beachhead, the Texans fought off a series of German counter-attacks, with vital support from the USAAF and the roaring offshore guns of the navy. During the next few days, the division advanced slowly, eventually securing the area from Agropoli to Altavilla. Altavilla was an old hilltop village, bristling with Germans. Overlooking the Gulf of Salerno, the settlement provided a great tactical advantage to whoever occupied it. On 13 September, the Texans stormed the village, taking it after a furious uphill struggle, and holding it against enemy counter-attacks. But the Germans managed to perform an outflanking manoeuvre and assault the village from the rear. The 36th Division was split by the enemy forces, and the order given to withdraw, though the Texans still in the village were completely surrounded and had to surrender.

This scenario allows you to play out an action that occurred as part of the Salerno landings, when an American force penetrated inland to secure high ground from the Axis defenders. Of course, you can adapt it for use in any World War II theatre, where a hilltop village has to taken from the enemy – a common occurrence as the Allies fought through Sicily and Italy.

FORCES

This scenario is designed to be played with equal points values on both sides. The Germans are the defenders in this scenario.

The following reinforced platoons should be used to represent the forces involved:

GERMANS
- Defence of Italy Reinforced Platoon (*Armies of Germany*, page 85).

USA
- Operation *Avalanche* Reinforced Platoon (*Armies of the United States*, page 63).

US troops pour into Italian territory in force.

SET-UP

TERRAIN

The table is set up as shown on the scenario map.

It's recommended you make a big hill for this scenario, covering an area about 36" x 24" – it should comprise of three semi-circular tiers, placed on top of each other to make two 3" steps leading up to the plateau at the top. This should give you enough space to place some buildings on top of the hill, representing the village. Along the curved edge of the topmost tier, the German player should place obstacles such as sandbags, barbed wire, etc.

Place a few bushes and trees on the tiers to represent the vine-covered slopes, which proved so difficult for the attackers to move through.

The rest of the table should be set up with a few woods, agricultural land, field boundaries such as hedges and walls, and maybe a small farm building.

DEPLOYMENT

The defender sets up half his force (rounding up, they can start the game hidden), on the topmost tier of the hill. Note that he cannot place any vehicles on the table at this stage. Any units not set up this way are held in reserve.

The attacker sets up at least half of his units in his set-up zone. Any units not set-up at this stage are held in reserve.

SPECIAL RULES

PREPARATORY BOMBARDMENT

The attacker rolls a die: on a 2+ a preparatory bombardment strikes the enemy positions. On a 1, the barrage fails to materialize, but you have your orders and the attack must go on as planned.

FIRST TURN

The battle begins.

ROUGH GOING

The vine-covered slopes of the hill make its ascent tough going – the lower two tiers count as rough ground and are impassable to all vehicles.

DEFENDER'S RESERVES

If the defender has any vehicles in reserve, these must be deployed as part of an outflanking manoeuvre.

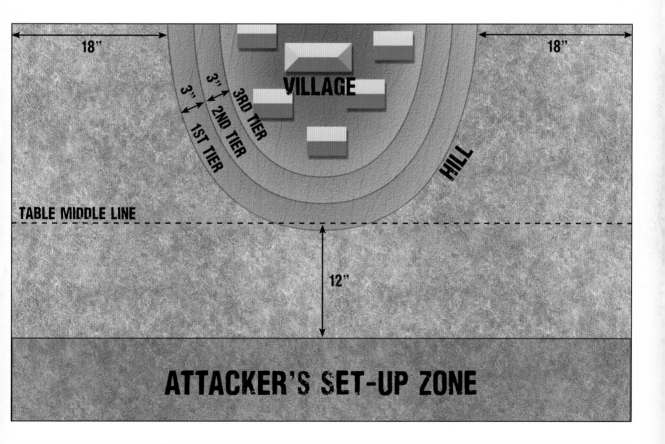

LEGENDS OF THE UNITED STATES

CHARLES 'COMMANDO' KELLY

Chuck 'Commando' Kelly (1920–85) was a United States Army soldier who received the Medal of Honor for his actions in the Italian campaign. Here is Kelly's official Medal of Honor citation:

"For conspicuous gallantry and intrepidity at risk of life above and beyond the call of duty. On 13 September 1943, near Altavilla, Italy, Cpl. Kelly voluntarily joined a patrol which located and neutralized enemy machine gun positions. After this hazardous duty he volunteered to establish contact with a battalion of US infantry which was believed to be located on Hill 315, a mile distant. He traveled over a route commanded by enemy observation and under sniper, mortar, and artillery fire; and later he returned with the correct information that the enemy occupied Hill 315 in organized positions. Immediately thereafter Cpl. Kelly, again a volunteer patrol member, assisted materially in the destruction of 2 enemy machinegun nests under conditions requiring great skill and courage. Having effectively fired his weapon until all the ammunition was exhausted, he secured permission to obtain more at an ammunition dump. Arriving at the dump, which was located near a storehouse on the extreme flank of his regiment's position, Cpl. Kelly found that the Germans were attacking ferociously at this point. He obtained his ammunition and was given the mission of protecting the rear of the storehouse. He held his position throughout the night. The following morning the enemy attack was resumed. Cpl. Kelly took a position at an open window of the storehouse. One machine gunner had been killed at this position and several other soldiers wounded. Cpl. Kelly delivered continuous aimed and effective fire upon the enemy with his automatic rifle until the weapon locked from overheating. Finding another automatic rifle, he again directed effective fire upon the enemy until this weapon also locked. At this critical point, with the enemy threatening to overrun the position, Cpl. Kelly picked up 60mm. mortar shells, pulled the safety pins, and used the shells as grenades, killing at least 5 of the enemy. When it became imperative that the house be evacuated, Cpl. Kelly, despite his sergeant's injunctions, volunteered to hold the position until the remainder of the detachment could withdraw. As the detachment moved out, Cpl. Kelly was observed deliberately loading and firing a rocket launcher from the window. He was successful in covering the withdrawal of the unit, and later in joining his own organization. Cpl. Kelly's fighting determination and intrepidity in battle exemplify the highest traditions of the U.S. Armed Forces."

Cost: +30pts

Team: He is not a team, but instead may be added to one of your Regular Infantry Squads (early, mid war), replacing the NCO, for the cost listed above.

Weapons: BAR automatic rifle (the unit can have a second BAR, purchasing it as normal).

Special Rules:

- Leader of men: Though he is just a Corporal, Commando Kelly confers his own unit a +4 morale bonus, just like a Major.

DUG-IN

The defenders can dig in. See page 124.

CONTROL OF THE SKIES

The Allies have control of the skies – see page 125.

OBJECTIVE

The attacker is trying to destroy the forces on the hill. The defender is trying to hold the hill at all costs.

GAME DURATION

Keep a count of how many turns have elapsed as the game is played. At the end of Turn 6, roll a die. On a result of 1, 2 or 3, the game ends, on a roll of 4, 5 or 6 play one further turn.

VICTORY!

The victory conditions are simple – if the defender has any units on the top tier of the hill (even partially) he has won – a vast wave of reinforcements arrives and pushes any attacking troops off the hill. If the defender has no units on the hill, the attacker wins. This might seem to be a difficult proposition for the attacker, but these types of fights were tough. The attacker has to really earn his victory in this scenario.

SCENARIO 14: THE RIVER RUNS RED – CROSSING THE RAPIDO

Here we have an action from the valiant US 36th Division again, this time along the defences that formed the Gustav Line. On 20 January 1944, Maj. Gen. Fred Walker of the 36th was ordered to cross the Rapido River (also known at this stretch as the Gari). Manoeuvring at night, the 141st Regiment and 143rd Regiment each got two battalions of men across, despite the dug-in positions of the 15th Panzer Grenadier Division. However, they were not provided with any armoured support, and the Germans made short and bloody work of them when day broke. By the evening of 22 January, the 141st was wiped out almost to a man. In all, the Texans lost over 2,000 men killed wounded and missing in this short and deadly confrontation.

The following scenario is designed to recreate this battle to cross the Rapido, though you can adapt it for use in any World War II theatre which involves an attacking army attempting to force its way across a major unbridged river. In the Italian campaign, you can equally well use this scenario (with a few tweaks) to represent the US crossing of the Volturno, and the British attack across the Garigliano, for example.

FORCES

This scenario is designed to be played with equal points values on both sides. The following reinforced platoons should be used to represent the forces involved:

GERMANS

- Defence of Italy Reinforced Platoon (*Armies of Germany*, page 85) – the German player has six free minefield sections (see Minefields, page 131).

USA

- Cassino Reinforced Platoon (*Armies of the United States*, page 64) – the entire force must start the game mounted in landing crafts, but all landing crafts are free (they count as Inexperienced – but you can pay extra points for them to improve their morale). The rules for all of these specialised units are found on page 135.

SET-UP

TERRAIN

The attacker's half of the table consists of deep water, while the defender's side is open ground, but should be littered with defences, as described below.

DEPLOYMENT

The German player places half of his forces (rounding up, they can start the game hidden), together with a good amount of obstacles like barbed wire, low walls, sandbag emplacements, tank traps and ditches, and up to three bunkers, within 12" of his table edge – this is his deployment area. Then he places his mines between 12" and 24" from his table edge. Any units not deployed are held back in reserve.

The attacker places no units at the start of the game. Instead he must nominate at least half his force as his first wave. Any units not included in the first wave are held back in reserve. To represent the lack of armoured support for the forces crossing the Rapido, the American player must place all his vehicles in reserve.

SPECIAL RULES

FIRST TURN

The battle begins. During Turn 1, the attacker must bring his entire first wave onto the table. These units can enter from any point on their table edge. Note that no order test is required to move units onto the table as part of the first wave.

DUG-IN

The German units deployed at the start of the game can all be dug-in (see page 124).

NIGHT FIGHTING

The attack takes place at night. If the US player wants a challenge, he can class it as a Dawn Assault. See the Night Fighting rules on page 129.

MUD

The battle is fought in the depths of winter, with almost perpetual, icy rain making the soldiers' lives a misery. The deluge has turned the battlefield into a sea of clinging mud. See page 136.

CONTROL OF THE SKIES

The Allies have control of the skies, but because of the torrential rain and low cloud, both sides count as having reduced airpower – see page 125.

AMPHIBIOUS ASSAULTS

This scenario uses the rules on page 134.

MINEFIELDS

This scenario uses the rules on page 131.

RESERVES

The attackers cannot use outflanking manoeuvres in this scenario. The defenders can only move outflanking units on up to the edge of the river, of course.

NO TANK SUPPORT

Had the 36th Division been given any armoured support, they might have stood a chance of holding their positions, and possible beating back the Germans. But none was forthcoming.

To represent this, not only the Modern Communications rule does not apply, but any vehicles in the American player's reserve require an order check with a –6 penalty to move on to the table!

OBJECTIVE

The attacking player must try to move as many of his units as he can into the defender's set-up zone and destroy the defending forces to establish a beachhead. The German player must try to stop him.

GAME DURATION

Keep a count of how many turns have elapsed as the game is played. At the end of Turn 6, roll a die. On a result of 1, 2 or 3 the game ends, on a roll of 4, 5 or 6 play one further turn.

VICTORY!

At the end of the game calculate which side has won by adding up victory points as follows. If one side scores at least 2 more points than the other then that side has won a clear victory. Otherwise, the result is a draw!

The attacking player scores 1 victory point for every enemy unit destroyed. He also scores 1 victory point for each of his own units that ends the game in the enemy deployment area and 2 victory points for each of his own unit that has moved off the enemy table edge before the end of the game.

The defending player scores 1 victory point for every enemy unit destroyed.

LEGENDS OF THE UNITED STATES

DANIEL KEN 'DAN' INOUYE

Daniel Ken 'Dan" Inouye (1924–2015) was a 'Nisei' – second generation Japanese American soldier – who received the Medal of Honor for his actions in the Italian campaign as part of the 442nd Regimental Combat Team. Here is Inouye's official Medal of Honor citation:

"Second Lieutenant Daniel K. Inouye distinguished himself by extraordinary heroism in action on 21 April 1945, in the vicinity of San Terenzo, Italy. While attacking a defended ridge guarding an important road junction, Second Lieutenant Inoue skilfully directed his platoon through a hail of automatic weapon and small arms fire, in a swift enveloping movement that resulted in the capture of an artillery and mortar post and brought his men to within 40 yards of the hostile force. Emplaced in bunkers and rock formations, the enemy halted the advance with crossfire from three machine guns. With complete disregard for his personal safety, Second Lieutenant Inouye crawled up the treacherous slope to within five yards of the nearest machine gun and hurled two grenades, destroying the emplacement. Before the enemy could retaliate, he stood up and neutralized a second machine gun nest. Although wounded by a sniper's bullet, he continued to engage other hostile positions at close range until an exploding grenade shattered his right arm. Despite the intense pain, he refused evacuation and continued to direct his platoon until enemy resistance was broken and his men were again deployed in defensive positions. In the attack, 25 enemy soldiers were killed and eight others captured. By his gallant, aggressive tactics and by his indomitable leadership, Second Lieutenant Inouye enabled his platoon to advance through formidable resistance, and was instrumental in the capture of the ridge. Second Lieutenant Inouye's extraordinary heroism and devotion to duty are in keeping with the highest traditions of military service and reflect great credit on him, his unit, and the United States Army."

Cost: 195pts (Veteran)

Team: 1 officer and up to 2 other men

Weapons: Dan Inouye is equipped with a submachine gun. Other men are equipped with submachine gun, pistol or rifle/carbine as depicted on the model.

Options:

• Inouye may be accompanied by up to 2 men at a cost of +13pts per man.

Special Rules:

• Lead by example: Inouye's Morale bonus is +4.

• Charge! If a US Veteran infantry squad within 6" of Inouye (including his own squad) is ordered to run towards (or charge) the closest visible enemy, any Order test for that move is automatically passed, as if the unit had rolled a double one. All models in the unit must then be moved directly towards one of the models in the target unit, and must make contact with the target unit if possible.

SCENARIO 15: BACKS TO THE SEA - ANZIO

Kesselring reacted with speed to the landings of the US VI Corps at Anzio. Using troops from Northern Italy, to avoid depleting the Gustav Line, he secured control of the strategically important Alban Hills and began to muster his forces to hurl the Allies back into the waves.

Four days after the landings, Major General Lucas was still consolidating his beachhead with no hurry to capture the high ground inland. He had effectively handed over the initiative to the enemy. On the ninth day of the landings, Lucas finally began to move out, just a day before his German counterpart, von Mackensen, was due to launch his counter-offensive. Overwhelming enemy resistance forced the Allies back. Lucas was exhausting his troops by throwing them against the well-entrenched German lines, so he called a halt to the attack and hunkered down to weather the German counter-attack.

On 16 February, the enemy struck. Powerful units from von Mackensen's 14th Army attacked along and either side of the Anzio-Albano road. His 1st Parachute Corp and LXXVII Panzer Corps pushed back the Allies, with the 26th Panzer and 29th Panzergrenadier Divisions waiting in the wings. Forced back to their final beachhead line, the US 3rd and 45th Infantry Divisions, the 1st Armored Brigade and the British 1st and 56th Divisions, supported by Special Forces units, could retreat no further, with their backs to the sea. They were saved from obliteration by the guns of the Navy off the coast of Anzio, and by Allied aircraft, which pounded the advancing Germans.

For five brutal days the battle raged, at close-quarters, with Lucas throwing in his reserves to plug breaches in the line. On the third day, the German reserves also entered the fray, but the massed barrage of the US artillery repelled them. The following day saw another German attack, but again they could not break through, and the Allies counter-attacked with tanks, pushing the enemy back a mile beyond their final defensive line. With his forces utterly exhausted, von Mackensen retired to lick his wounds, leaving the Allied beachhead badly battered but still functioning.

The following scenario allows you to recreate the Allies' desperate battle for survival at Anzio, and the determined German effort to push the invaders into the sea. The action takes place on the fourth day, with the defending Allies already having used up their last reserves.

You can adapt this scenario for use in any World War II theatre where a fragile beachhead is under assault.

FORCES

This scenario is designed to be played with equal points values on both sides. The following reinforced platoons should be used to represent the forces involved:

GERMANS
• Defence of Italy Reinforced Platoon (*Armies of Germany*, page 85).

USA
• Anzio, the Road to Rome Reinforced Platoon (*Armies of the United States*, page 65)

BRITISH & COMMONWEALTH
• Monte Cassino Reinforced Platoon (*Armies of Great Britain*, page 72)

Note – the Allies are well supported with both artillery from the offshore navy and from the air. To represent this, a US force has both types of forward observers (artillery and air) for free, while a British force has a free air observer as well as its normal artillery observer.

SET-UP

TERRAIN
Set up the terrain as shown on the scenario map, with the Anzio/Albano road bisecting the table along the centre, from long edge to long edge. There should be plenty of buildings on the tabletop, representing the town of Anzio. The buildings should be more plentiful and closer spaced on the Allied side of the table, with fewer and more spaced out buildings on the Axis side. Most of the buildings in this area of the conflict should be rubble, reduced by the fighting of the last few days, and moving through them counts as rough ground.

The Allied player is the defender and can set up obstacles, such as sandbag ramparts, barbed wire and gun emplacements, anywhere within his set-up zone.

DEPLOYMENT
The Allied player sets up his entire force first, within his set-up zone.

The German player then sets up at least half of his units within his set-up zone. Any units not deployed at this stage are in reserve.

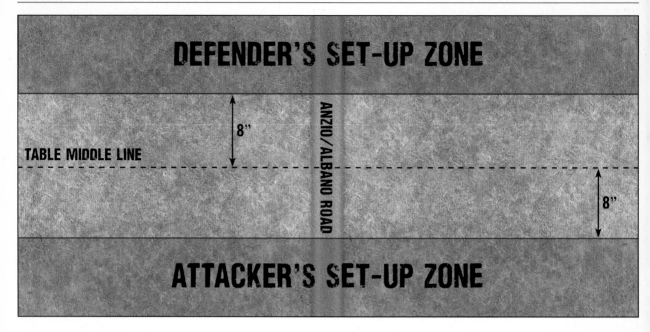

DEFENDER'S SET-UP ZONE

8"

TABLE MIDDLE LINE

ANZIO/ALBANO ROAD

8"

ATTACKER'S SET-UP ZONE

SPECIAL RULES

PREPARATORY BOMBARDMENT

The attacker rolls a die: on a 2+ a preparatory bombardment strikes the enemy positions. On a 1, the barrage fails to materialize.

To represent the presence of the Allies' naval artillery positioned offshore, and the strength of the Allied air support, a preparatory bombardment now automatically strikes the Axis positions.

FIRST TURN

The battle begins.

MULTINATIONAL FORCES

Feel free to use these rules for mixed Allied forces. The rules are on page 120.

DUG-IN

The defenders can dig in. See page 124.

CONTROL OF THE SKIES

The Allies have control of the skies – see page 125.

AMERICAN-LED OPERATION

To represent the domination of the US Army in this operation, if the Allied player is using a British, or mixed British/American force, all air observers gain the US Army special rule, Air Power (*Bolt Action* page 146).

NAVY GUNS

To represent the power of the offshore Navy guns, an Allied player fielding an American force gains the Bombardment special rule (*Bolt Action* page 160).

BACKS TO THE SEA

The pressure from the German attack has been relentless for four days now, and exhaustion is setting in for the defenders. All defending units on the tabletop at the start of the battle begin the game with 1 pin marker.

RESERVES

Neither side can use outflanking manoeuvres in this game – both sides must face each other head on.

OBJECTIVE

The Germans must obliterate the enemy. The Allies must try to hold the line – they have nowhere else to run to!

GAME DURATION

Keep a count of how many turns have elapsed as the game is played. At the end of Turn 6, roll a die. On a result of 1, 2 or 3 the game ends, on a roll of 4, 5 or 6 play one further turn.

VICTORY!

At the end of the game, calculate which side has won by adding up victory points as follows. If one side scores at least 2 more victory points than the other then that side has won a clear victory. Otherwise the result is deemed too close to call and honours are shared – a draw!

Players score 1 victory point for every enemy unit destroyed.

SCENARIO 16: MONTE CASSINO – ATTEMPT ON MONASTERY HILL

On 17 February, 1944, Brigadier Lovett of 7th Indian Brigade, a unit of the II New Zealand Corps, was ordered by his commander, Lieutenant-General Freyberg, to make a direct attack on Monte Cassino. This action was part of the second attempt to wrest control of the imposing heights of Monastery Hill from the Germans – the first battle, fought by the US II Corps and French Expeditionary Corps, had ended in stalemate the month before. Lovett lead the 4th/6th Rajputana Rifles, the 1st/2nd Gurkhas and the 1st/9th Gurkhas against enemy strongpoints ensconced on the hilltops to the north-west of the monastery. Two days earlier, Allied bombers had reduced the monastery to rubble, under the mistaken belief that it was occupied by German troops, and nearby positions had also taken a pounding. By now, though, the defenders had recovered from the onslaught, and pinned down the attackers as they traversed the bare mountainside. Although the 1st/2nd Gurkhas managed to reach a ravine at the base of Monastery Hill, they were beaten back by sheer enemy firepower while trying to climb up to the abbey. The Allied troops were forced to retreat, their dead littering the rocky landscape.

This scenario is based on the attack on Monastery Hill at Monte Cassino, but you can adapt it for use in any World War II theatre where an attacking force has been ordered to assault an almost impregnable mountaintop enemy position.

FORCES

This scenario is designed to be played with equal points values on both sides. The following reinforced platoons should be used to represent the forces involved:

GERMANS

- Defence of Italy Reinforced Platoon (*Armies of Germany*, page 85) – The Germans are the defenders in this game. They can purchase minefield sections at 50pts each but cannot spend more than 10% of their force total on minefields (see page 131).

BRITISH & COMMONWEALTH

- Indian Division Reinforced Platoon (page 23) – Indian and Gurkha troops were involved in this fight – you must take at least one Infantry Section to represent the Indians, and one Gurkha Infantry Section. Other Infantry Sections must be either Indians or Gurkhas.

Italian infantry prepare to take back an enemy-held village

Note that because of the mountainous terrain, neither side can take any vehicles.

SET-UP
TERRAIN
Set up the table as shown on the scenario map.

The Allied set-up zone is anywhere up to 24" away from the north corner of the Allied table edge.

The main feature of the battlefield is the huge hill representing Monastery Hill – you can use the same piece of terrain to represent this as was used for the hill in the Assault on Altavilla scenario (page 104). Note that this hill has three tiers – these are important for the game's victory conditions, as described below.

One steep 24" x 12" hill (Point 593) is placed in the north-west corner of the battlefield. Two less steep 12" x 12" hills are also needed, one (Point 445) placed near the middle of the north-east long table edge (12" from the Allied set-up zone), the other (Point 444) placed near the middle of the opposite long table edge (no closer than 6" from the hills flanking it). A narrow ravine, about 24" long, should be put at the bottom of

Monastery Hill, about 12" from either long table edge (you can represent this quite simply with card cut to shape, unless you're an accomplished model terrain maker).

The entire tabletop, including the hills, should be scattered with boulders and rocks to give the attackers at least some cover. Otherwise, the battlefield should be bare of any other natural features. The German player should place plenty of defensive obstacles (barbed wire, machine-gun or mortar emplacements, etc.) on all the hills, including Monastery Hill.

You don't have to feature the abbey itself – we can say it's just off the south-east short edge of the board. However, if you have any ruined fortress walls, you can place these on the top of Monastery Hill within 6" of the short table edge to represent one of the abbey's cyclopean (but now utterly destroyed) walls.

DEPLOYMENT

The German player sets up all his units on the table, on any hill. All his units can be hidden at the start of the game.

The Allied player sets up at least half of his force within his set-up zone. Any units not deployed at this stage are in reserve.

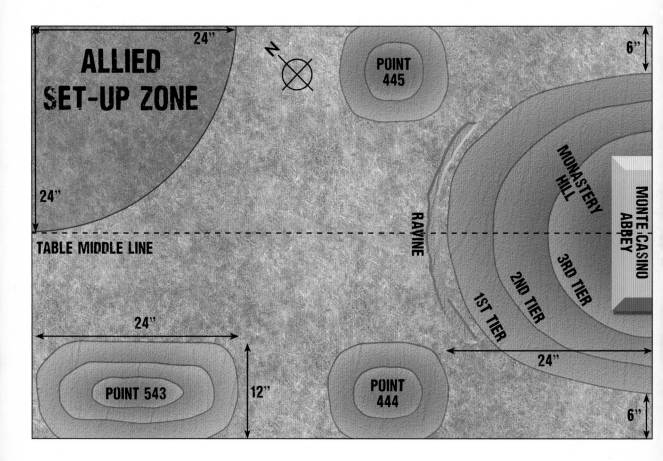

SPECIAL RULES

FIRST TURN
The battle begins.

DUG-IN
Although the ground is hard and rocky, the defenders can dig in – this represents the troops piling up rocks in front of themselves to create a low, makeshift wall. See page 124.

CONTROL OF THE SKIES
The Allies have control of the skies – see page 125.

MINEFIELDS
The defenders are allowed to place minefields. See page 131.

RAVINE
The ravine is impassable to all models.

ROUGH TERRAIN
The battle is fought high up near the mountain summit on top of which the abbey of Monte Cassino is perched. As such, although the rocky ground is not affected by the mud afflicting the troops down in the valley below, its steep, boulder-strewn landscape means the entire battlefield counts as rough ground and impassable to all vehicles.

However, the Gurkhas, hailing as they do from the mountains of Nepal, are experts at fighting in this type of highland terrain, so do not count the battlefield as rough ground.

RESERVES
Allied reserves can enter the tabletop from any point up to 24" from the north corner of the battlefield. Outflanking manoeuvres cannot be made.

OBJECTIVE
The Allied player must try to get one or more units as far up Monastery Hill as possible by the end of the game. The German player must try to stop him doing this.

GAME DURATION
Keep a count of how many turns have elapsed as the game is played. At the end of Turn 8, roll a die. On a result of 1, 2 or 3 the game ends, on a roll of 4, 5 or 6 play one further turn.

VICTORY!
At the end of the game, calculate which side has won by adding up victory points as follows. If one side scores at least 2 more victory points than the other then that side has won a clear victory. Otherwise the result is deemed too close to call and honours are shared – a draw!

The Allied player scores 1 victory point for every enemy unit destroyed. He also scores a number of victory points depending on which tier of Monastery Hill his troops have ascended. 1 victory point per units on the first tier; 2 victory points per unit on the second tier; 3 victory points per unit on the third tier.

The German player scores 2 victory points for every enemy unit destroyed.

German troops storm the grounds of an Italian villa

SCENARIO 17: THE GOTHIC LINE – WAR OF ATTRITION

"The Battle of Rimini was one of the hardest battles of the Eight Army. The fighting was comparable to El Alamein, Mareth and the Gustav Line." – Lt.-Gen. Sir Oliver Leese, Commander of the 8th Army.

On 3 September, 1944, the I Canadian Corps, comprising of the 1st Canadian infantry Division supported by the British 21st Army Tank Brigade, with the 5th Canadian Armoured Division in reserve, attacked the second perimeter of German defences along the Gothic Line. They had already overrun the first line several days previously, after crossing the Foglio River. Buoyed by this success, they came close to breaking the enemy positions again, until a fierce German artillery barrage, accompanied by a timely counter-attack by paratroopers from the LXXVI Panzer Corps halted the Canadians' assault.

The following scenario represents the Canadian attack on the fortifications of the Gothic Line. Of course, you can adapt it for use in any World War II theatre where the attackers have to forge a path through heavily fortified enemy positions.

FORCES

This scenario pitches a larger attacking force against a smaller, well-defended enemy force. The German player picks a force to an agreed points value, and the Allied player picks a force total of three times that amount.

The following reinforced platoons should be used to represent the forces involved:

GERMANS
• Defence of Italy Reinforced Platoon (Armies of Germany, page 85).

BRITISH & COMMONWEALTH
• Monte Cassino Reinforced Platoon (*Armies of Great Britain*, page 72).

SET-UP

TERRAIN

In addition to his force, the German player receives three bunkers, nine 'hard cover' linear obstacles and two minefield sections (see page 131 for rules on minefields). Each linear obstacle must be 6" long and 1" tall, and should provide hard cover (so use trenches, low walls, earth embankments,

sandbags, etc.). You can replace any number of 'hard cover' linear obstacles with 'soft cover' ones (e.g. barbed wire). If you do so, you get two 'soft cover' obstacles for each 'hard cover' one you surrender.

Bunkers must be large enough to accommodate a single unit of infantry or artillery. The rules for bunkers are on page 104 of the *Bolt Action* rulebook.

The German player sets up one of his bunkers and three linear obstacles in each of the areas highlighted in red on the scenario map – the first, second and third defence lines. Both minefields must be placed so that they are between the first and second defence lines – they may be combined into a single mixed minefield if desired.

The rest of the table should have reasonably sparse terrain like copses of trees, hillocks or rock outcroppings to impede movement. As the tabletop represents a prepared line of defence, anything likely to provide much cover to an attacker will have been removed to leave a good field of fire to the troops in the bunkers and behind the fortifications.

The last strip of table between the third defence line and the Defender's edge of the table can include heavier terrain, like woodland.

DEPLOYMENT

The German player divides the number of units in his army by three. The result is the number of units that must be deployed within each defence line. Of course, unless the total number of units in your army is a multiple of three, you'll end up with one or two spare units – these can be placed in any defence line or left in reserve (they can even outflank!). For example, if you have seven units, you must place two in each defence line and you end up with a spare one, which you can add to any defence line or leave in reserve. Defending units can (and should!) use the Dug-In and Hidden set-up Rules (see Hidden Set-up on page 117 of the *Bolt Action* rulebook and the Dug-In rules on page 124 of this book).

The Allied units are not set-up on the table at the start of the game. The Allied player must nominate half of his force (rounding up) to form his first wave. Any units not included in the first wave are left in reserve. Allied units in reserve cannot outflank in this scenario, and similarly units with special deployment rules, like snipers, observers and spotters, cannot use their special deployment.

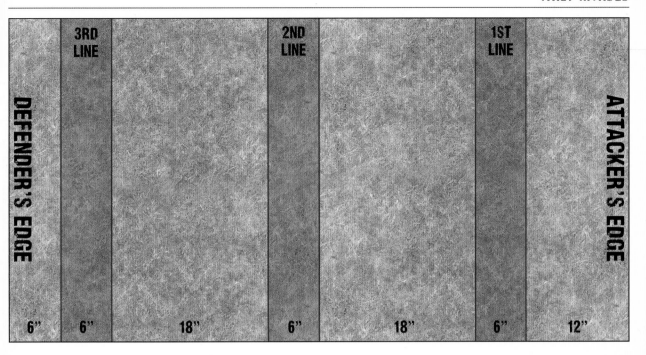

SPECIAL RULES

PREPARATORY BOMBARDMENT

The Allied player rolls a die: on a 2+, a preparatory bombardment strikes the enemy positions (see Preparatory Bombardment on page 118 of the *Bolt Action* rulebook). On a result of 1, the barrage fails to appear.

FIRST TURN

Once the battle begins, the attacker must move his first wave onto the table during Turn 1. These units can enter the table from any point on the attacker's table edge, and must be given either a *run* or *advance* order. Note that no order test is required to move units onto the table as part of the first wave, and remember that they cannot assault on the turn they enter the table.

DUG-IN

The defenders can dig in. See page 124.

CONTROL OF THE SKIES

The Allies have control of the skies – see page 125.

MINEFIELDS

See page 131.

LIMITED FUEL SUPPLY

The Limited Fuel Supply rules (page 133) affects the German player – Allied bombing raids and Partisan sabotage are choking the German's access to supplies.

SHODDY CONSTRUCTION

The apparent impregnability of the Gothic Line was undermined by the fact that the tons of concrete used to build its fortifications was extremely poor quality, the result of using 15,000 slave labourers for the construction, and of sabotage by Italian partisans.

To represent this, any bunkers used in this scenario only have a cover modifier of –3 (instead of the usual –4), and indirect fire weapons, which usually have no effect on the occupants of bunkers, penetrate the bunker on the D6 score of a 6.

OBJECTIVE

The Allied player must try to capture the three bunkers – the German player must try to stop him. To capture a bunker, the attacker needs to clear it of all enemies and enter it at some point during the game with one of his infantry units. If the German player moves an infantry unit back in, then the Allied player must capture it again.

GAME DURATION

Keep a count of how many turns have elapsed as the game is played. At the end of Turn 10, roll a die. On a result of 1, 2 or 3 the game ends, on a roll of 4, 5 or 6 play one further turn.

VICTORY!

At the end of the game, if the Allied player has captured all three bunkers he wins. If the Allied player has captured two bunkers the game is a draw. If the Allied player has captured one bunker (or none!) then the German player wins.

All bunkers are held by the German player at the start of the game regardless of where his troops are positioned. If a bunker changes hands during the game then it remains under the control of that side until it is taken back.

To capture a bunker there must be no enemy in it and you must move one of your infantry units inside it.

ADDITIONAL UNITS

UNITED STATES

VETERAN INFANTRY SQUAD

Due to the relatively short amount of time at the front, and particularly because of the constant influx of replacements, regular US infantry units never got quite as 'seasoned' as those of some other countries that lacked the American manpower, training and organisation. Nevertheless, some regular Army units did fight on enough fronts to become true veterans, like the famous Big Red One (1st Infantry Division), or the ultra-decorated Nisei units, renowned for their courage and stubbornness under fire.

Cost: 78pts (Veteran)
Composition: 1 NCO and 5 men
Weapons: M1 Garand rifles
Options:
- Add up to 6 additional men with rifles for +13pts each.
- The NCO and up to three additional men can have submachine guns instead of their rifles at a cost of +3pts each.
- Up to 2 men can have a BAR M1918A2 automatic rifle instead of a rifle for +5pts each.
- The squad can be given anti-tank grenades for +2pts per man
- Any veteran infantry squad can be Tough Fighters for +1pt per man
Special Rules:
- Tank hunters (if anti-tank grenades taken)
- Tough fighters (if option is taken)

SELECTORS

The Veteran Infantry Squad is an Infantry Squad for the purposes of the generic Reinforced Platoon selector from the *Bolt Action* rulebook. It is also an Infantry Squad for the following theatre selectors of the *Armies of the United States* book: Operation *Husky*; Operation *Avalanche*; Cassino; Anzio, the road to Rome; Normandy; Operation *Cobra*; Operation *Market Garden*; Battle of the Bulge; Bastogne; Operation *Grenade*; Rhineland.

M29 WEASEL

The M29 Weasel was a tracked vehicle designed by the US automobile manufacturer, Studebaker. Originally conceived as a fast mode of transport for commando units operating in snowy terrain, it saw active service throughout Europe wherever difficult ground immobilised wheeled vehicles. The M29 was not amphibious, but a specialised amphibious version (the M29C Water Weasel) was also available.

Cost: 52pts (Inexperienced), 65pts (Regular), 78pts (Veteran).
Weapons: None
Damage Value: 7+ (armoured carrier)
Transport: 5 men
Tow: light antitank gun, light howitzer, light anti-aircraft gun
Options:
- Make Amphibious (M29C Water Weasel) for +5pts
Special Rules:
- Open topped
- Recce
- Turn on the spot – the Weasel can turn on the spot enabling it to execute a full speed run rate 'reverse', finishing the move facing in the direction of travel.

US infantry squad with M3 half-track

SELECTORS

The Weasel counts as a transport or tow for the purposes of the generic Reinforced Platoon selector from the *Bolt Action* rulebook. Alternatively, it can be added to any US selector from 1942 onwards.

ITALY

LATE-WAR *PARACADUTISTI* (PARATROOPERS) INFANTRY SECTION

This entry covers late-war units of Italian paratroopers, like the newly formed Nembo division that took part in the defence of Anzio and Rome, and the units that kept fighting on both sides until the end of the war.

Cost: Veteran Infantry 70pts.
Composition: 1 NCO and 4 men
Weapons: Rifles
Options:

- Add up to 5 additional soldiers at +14pts each
- The NCO can replace his rifle with a pistol for −3pts, or a submachine gun for +3pts, or an assault rifle for +5pts
- Any man can replace his rifle with a submachine gun for +3 points each
- One man can have a light machine gun for +20pts – another man becomes the loader.
- Up to 3 men can have a Panzerfaust in addition to other weapons for +5pts each.
- The entire section can be given anti-tank grenades for +2 points per man

Special Rules:

- Stubborn. Paratroops don't give in easily! If forced to check their morale when reduced to half strength then they always test on their full morale value ignoring any pin markers.
- Tank hunters (if anti-tank grenades taken).

SELECTORS

The Late War *Paracadutisti* count as an infantry squad for the purposes of the generic Reinforced Platoon selector from the *Bolt Action* rulebook. Alternatively, they can be added to selectors for scenarios set in Italy between the defence of Anzio and the end of the war.

SEMOVENTE 75/34

After the relative success of the Semovente 75/18, work begun on a new version with a slightly improved frontal armour and, more importantly, a more powerful anti-tank gun. The result – the Semovente 75/34 – was produced in only around 60 units before the Italian surrender and the German taking over of the factories. The occupying Germans requisitioned some of these vehicles and continued their production for their own use for the rest of the war.

Cost: 176pts (Inexperienced), 220pts (Regular), 244pts (Veteran)
Weapons: 1 forward facing hull-mounted heavy anti-tank gun, 1 forward-facing hull-mounted MMG
Damage Value: 9+ (medium tank)
Special Rules:

- Vulnerable: because of the riveted construction, all shots to the side and rear of the vehicle get an additional +1 penetration modifier (i.e. in total, +2 for side hits and +3 for rear hits).
- HE: Instead of causing D2 HE hits, an HE shell causes D6 hits.

SELECTORS

The 75/34 are self-propelled guns for the purposes of the generic Reinforced Platoon selector from the *Bolt Action*. Alternatively, they can be added to selectors for scenarios set in Italy between the defence of Anzio and the end of the war.

Late-war Italian paratrooper section

THEATRE SELECTORS

POST-ARMISTICE ITALIAN ARMED FORCES

After the armistice, the King of Italy and the new prime minister, Pietro Badoglio, who had fled to the Allied-control south after the German invasion, ordered that the *Regio Esercito* was to fight against their former German comrades on the side of the Allied.

A few days later, Mussolini also reappeared, after having been liberated by German special forces and re-instated as the leader of the puppet state of the *Repubblica Sociale Italiana* with headquarters in Salò on Lake Garda. The *Duce* ordered his former troops to regroup and continue the fight on the side of the Germans.

As one can imagine, these conflicting orders proved very confusing and extremely controversial with different units and officers of the Italian armed forces. The troops in the German-controlled north had been disarmed at gunpoint by the Germans – some had resisted and had been killed, many had been deported to other territories of the Reich as slave labour. Some of the remaining soldiers decided to heed the call of Mussolini and re-enlisted to fight for him and alongside the Germans. Some simply melted in the civilian population and went into hiding. Others, animated by political views diametrically opposed to the Fascists', or simply as a reaction to the brutality of the German occupation, joined the resistance, swelling the partisan armies in the mountains of northern Italy.

Particularly tragic was the fate of several Italian units that were fighting abroad or were occupying areas of the Balkans and the Aegean. Some units surrendered to their former allies and were interned in prison and labour camps. Some resisted, and were often annihilated before any help could come to them from the Allies – such as on the island of Cephalonia, where over 5000 Italian prisoners of war were massacred by the Germans.

In the Allied-controlled south, the soldiers that were to fight alongside the Allies as the Italian Co-belligerent Army were reorganized after the chaos that had followed the armistice. They were first employed by the Allies in attacks against the Gustav line near Cassino. Having proven their allegiance, the units were then used for the rest of the Italian campaign, and some units were re-equipped and re-trained by the British. Fighting alongside the Gothic line saw Italian units fighting on both sides. Below, we listed a set of guidelines for using Italian troops after the armistice of 8 September 1943.

ITALIAN CO-BELLIGERENT ARMY REINFORCED PLATOONS

To represent forces immediately following the armistice, for scenarios set along the Gustav line, Rome, etc., pick platoons as normal from the generic Reinforced Platoon on page 10 of the *Armies of Italy and the Axis* book, except that you cannot have Colonial Troops, *Camicie Nere* (Blackshirts) and Autoblinda Lince. These platoons can be fielded in multinational forces alongside US or British platoons.

To represent later troops engaged against the Gothic line and at the very end of the war, you can instead pick platoons from the *Armies of Great Britain*, using the Monte Cassino selector. In this case assume that the infantry is Italians fighting in British gear and using British doctrine, with the vehicles and some of the officers actually being British (and more importantly, the artillery observers!).

In this case it is characterful to either use the *Vengeance* National Characteristic or to instead replace the National Characteristic with the *Avanti Savoia!* Italian army special rule.

REPUBBLICA SOCIALE ITALIANA REINFORCED PLATOONS

Pick platoons as normal from the generic Reinforced Platoon on page 10 of the *Armies of Italy and the Axis* book, except that you cannot have Colonial Troops. Some of the vehicles in the Italian army list (like the Semovente 90/53) were probably not used by *Repubblica Sociale* forces, but as the records for his period are obviously confused, you can use them all, and just assume that some might have German crewmen (but this makes no difference in game terms).

In addition, one unit of *Camicie Nere* (Blackshirts) can replace the *Non Testati* special rule with the Fanatics special rules for +3pts per man.

These platoons can be used in a multinational force with German Platoons from the *Defence of Italy* selector for actions alongside the Gothic line. Alternatively, you could use them alongside German forces from the Anti-partisan Security Patrol selector in a game against a Partisan force.

ITALIAN PARTISANS REINFORCED PLATOONS

Pick a partisan force as normal from the *Armies of France and the Allies* book. It can be interesting to give the partisans the *Avanti Savoia!* special rule to make the partisan force more unique and characterfully Italian, as that rule is fairly neutral in terms of game balance.

NEW SCENARIO RULES

2nd Battalion, 1st Fallschirmjäger Regiment landing just west of Heraklion airfield on the afternoon of 20 May 1941, by Howard Gerrard © Osprey Publishing Ltd. Taken from Campaign 147: Crete 1941.

MULTINATIONAL FORCES

"Allies must fight in desperate theatres or they hate each other more than the enemy." – General Patton

It was common for units of different allied nationalities to be deployed to separate sectors to avoid communication problems. However, in the heat of battle it often happened that troops would find themselves fighting shoulder to shoulder with the forces of allied nations. These rules offer an optional way to mix nationalities within your force.

First of all, we encourage mixing forces only with both sides' agreement, as mixed forces may occasionally trigger rules conflicts, which will need to be resolved on the fly by the players. As a guideline, special rules that affect a force or units of one nationality do not affect their allies. For example, the Morale bonus of a British officer would not affect US units, and the Modern Communications army special rule of the Americans does not affect British units that are in Reserve alongside their US counterparts.

When assembling a mixed force, select at least one platoon from one army list (e.g. *Armies of the United States*) and then at least one platoon from another army list (e.g. *Armies of Great Britain*). The points cost total of all of these platoons added together must be equal to the agreed point total, in other words equal to the opponent's total. For example, if you are about to face 1,000pts of Germans, you may want to select one or more US platoons to a value of 500pts and one or more British platoons to a value of 500pts. Of course the split does not have to be 50–50, we leave that to the players (e.g. a larger Italian force may include a smaller German contingent in a scenario set in North Africa).

The same player can control these different nationalities' platoons if you wish. However, we definitely think it's more entertaining if each nationality's forces are controlled by a separate player.

If you are using theatre selectors to pick those platoons, it is best if you pick forces that make sense together – for example an American platoon from the 1943 – Rommel's Defeat selector in the Armies of the US would go well together with a British platoon from the 1942–43 – Tunisia selector in the *Armies of Great Britain*.

During the game, you may use the same colour dice for the entire mixed force, in which case you'll have to decide which unit gets the dice – or debate it with your allied player!

Alternatively, you may assign different coloured dice to each nationality, which will speed up things considerably. This is by far our favourite solution.

At the end of a game, each nationality scores victory points individually (which gives you bragging rights), but the forces fighting as allies will of course add their points together to calculate which side has won the game, as normal.

For any multi-player game set in the North African and Italian theatres that involves Allied Multinational forces, we recommend that the American player's main objective is to score more victory points than their British counterpart. This represents the rivalry between the Allied generals, which influenced events such as Patton's obsession to reach Messina before Montgomery and General Mark Clark's decision to refuse a direct order from General Alexander, his superior officer, to envelop Germans retreating from the Gustav line, and instead send his army to capture Rome, which won him personal glory but allowed the Germans to escape and reinforce the Gothic Line.

French Foreign Legion squad

DESERT WARFARE

Most of the North African battles featured in this supplement involve battles in the desert, and here we provide rules to replicate the challenges of fighting in such an extreme and hostile environment. Use any or all of the following rules for games played in a desert region.

DESERT TERRAIN

You might think that setting up boards for wargaming in a desert region would be straightforward: paint up some MDF sandy-yellow then just deploy your troops on the flat, featureless tabletop. However, as well as promising a fairly uninteresting game, this also does not reflect the realities of desert warfare.

Typical examples of desert terrain would be low, one or two-tier, hills (open ground) or sandy dunes and one or two rocky outcrops (rough ground), interspersed with low natural ditches and the odd man-made drystone wall (obstacles). You'll find that these meagre sources of cover will be fiercely fought over as troops attempt to secure them for protection.

There might be a few patches of rocky terrain (rough ground) on the battlefield, plus areas of very soft sand (rough ground). Tracked vehicles roll a D6 as soon as they come into contact with this area. On a 4+ they can move through normally, otherwise they can only move a maximum distance equal to the number they rolled (i.e. 1, 2 or 3 inches)). An area of soft sand should be painted a more yellow shade than the colour of the game board, to make it stand out.

Your tabletop might be spanned by a wadi – in the rainy season (the Autumn months) it will be a fast flowing watercourse (impassable except at a crossing point) flanked by bushes and other foliage. The rest of the year the water will flow underground, and the wadi will be a dry, rocky valley (rough ground).

The desert is dotted here and there with the odd oasis – an impassable pool of water surrounded by lush vegetation and palm trees. There should be no more than one of these on the tabletop (perhaps you can only place an oasis on the D6 score of a 6 to represent its rarity).

The desert is sparsely populated, and then mainly with nomadic Arab tribesmen. Settlements are few and far between, but as such can be vital for the lifeline of an army traversing the desert, and so can be the common focus of desert battles. Native villages tend to comprise of squat, square, flat-roofed adobe huts.

If the battle is being fought along one of the few highways between major settlements, a road could cross the battlefield. This will be very poorly maintained, so a vehicle moving along it can only double its move rate on the D6 score of a 4+, otherwise it becomes hampered by potholes.

Italians recce in the North African desert.

DIGGING IN

The soft sand of the desert makes it easy for troops to excavate protective foxholes and trenches. All scenarios fought in a desert allow the use of the Dug-in rules (see page 124).

CLIMATE CONDITIONS

Desert fighting has its own unique complications caused by the sun-baked, featureless, sandy landscape. These are reflected by the following special rules:

DESERT FIGHTERS

Any unit that is part of a force fighting in the desert can be given the Desert Fighters special rule at the cost of +2pts per man. The unit has learned how to become adept at mitigating the worst effects of fighting in the desert, and ignores all the climate conditions described below.

HOT, DAMN HOT

Infantry can easily become dehydrated while fighting in the soaring temperatures of the desert. Except at dawn or at night, infantry units in the desert must roll a D6 if given a Run order. If the result is less than the current game turn, that unit is suffering from the effects of dehydration and can only move up to 6" (though still counts as running). A unit does not have to take this test if it is within 6" of a water source (e.g. an oasis, village well, provisions dump, etc.).

SAND, SAND...

Sand clogs vehicles' fuel lines, wears out tires and other rubber parts, and seeps into engines and cooling systems, resulting in overheated engines. Higher maintenance than usual is required at all times to avoid this. To represent this, vehicles (and infantry with the Motorbike special rule) operating in battles fought in a desert region are subject to the Unreliable rule:

- **Unreliable:** If the unit suffers one or more pin markers as a result of an enemy attack, it automatically suffers one further pin marker in addition.

...AND MORE SAND

Sand also gets into gun barrels and firing mechanisms, causing frequent stoppages. Coupled with the fact that the lack of visible features, the strong sun glare or billowing dust clouds make accurate range estimations difficult, this has a serious effect on ranged combat. Vehicles and artillery units fighting in a desert region suffer a –2 to hit penalty when shooting at long range, instead of the normal –1.

ENVIRONMENTAL EFFECTS

At any moment, localised environmental effects can suddenly occur, making fighting in the desert even more challenging. Note that the effects described below even affect units with the Desert Fighters special rule.

BLINDSIDE

The best time to launch an offensive in the desert is when the sun is low and behind the attackers. The rising sun's rays will dazzle the defenders, giving the attackers a big advantage. Of course, a wise commander will try to position his defences in such a way to avoid this. Use the following rules for battles set in the desert that involve a Dawn Assault (see page 129):

- After the set-up phase, each player rolls a D6 and adds the Officer Morale modifier of their force's commanding officer (i.e. the highest ranking officer). If a player's commanding officer has the Desert Fighter special rule, that player can re-roll the die if he wishes. If the attacker scores at least twice the score of the defender, he has successfully coordinated his attack so that the sun is behind his troops.
- The player chooses one table edge. This represents the position of the sun during the battle. Any unit firing in the direction of that table edge is firing into the rays of the sun and suffers an additional –1 penalty to rolls to hit. A unit is firing 'in the direction of the table edge' if a line can be drawn from any of the firing models towards the table edge crossing the base/hull of any of the models in the target unit.

DUST TRAIL

Advancing vehicles cause dust clouds that can be seen for miles around across the flat desert. Use the following rule for games set in a desert region where the attacker has at least one vehicle or unit with the Cavalry or Motorbike special rule:

- If the scenario being played specifically involves an attacker and defender, the defender can choose to return the first order die drawn for that game and draw again. This represents the advantage the defender has from seeing the attacker approach at a long distance. Note that if visibility is limited due to Haze, or the Reduced Visibility rules are in play (see below), the Dust Trail effect is ignored.

WEATHER EFFECTS

At the start of a game set in the desert, before the set-up phase, each player rolls a D6. If they roll an identical score, refer to the Weather Table to determine what weather effects affect the battlefield.

WEATHER EFFECTS TABLE

SCORE	EFFECT
1–2	**Something's brewing on the horizon:** No immediate effect, but at the end of each game turn, one player must roll D6+1 and refer to this table. He doesn't continue rolling on this table after a weather effect has taken place.
3–4	**Haze:** The intense temperature causes a heat haze to blur the horizon. All weapons firing at a distance greater than 12" count as firing at long range, regardless of their Range. In addition, when rolling on one of the Barrage tables (Bolt Action page 64), a player must roll two D6 and choose the lowest score as his result.
5	**Mirage:** As Haze, above. In addition, any unit that fails an order test on ANY double (not just double 6) suffers a FUBAR. This represents the panic and confusion of units misinterpreting desert mirages for enemy movement.
6	**Sandstorm:** Fierce winds rage across the desert, whipping up sand into swirling tornados that obscure visibility and pin down anyone foolish to be out abroad. At the start of a game turn where a sandstorm is on the battlefield, each infantry and artillery unit that does not have the majority of its models within terrain, or is not dug-in (see page 124) immediately gains D3–1 pin markers. This represents the disorientating, blasting effect of the sandstorm. In addition, while a sandstorm is raging, all units on the table are affected by the Limited Visibility rules (see page 130). At the end of each game turn where a sandstorm is on the battlefield, one player rolls a D6. On a 6+ the sandstorm dies down and has no further effect on the game. As soon as a sandstorm strikes the battlefield, the Desert Fighters special rule has no effect for the rest of the game – sand gets everywhere confounding the best efforts of even the most well-prepared desert fighter. This means units with the Desert Fighter rule are now affected by all of the rules detailed above.

THE FOG OF WAR

As the tide of battle churns up the soft desert sand, dust clouds envelope the battlefield, quickly hampering visibility. During a battle fought in the desert, when a vehicle makes a Run move, its controller rolls a D6. On a 4, 5 or 6, he places a 4" diameter 'dust cloud' marker adjacent to the rear of the vehicle (using cotton wool, especially the yellow coloured stuff, is ideal to represent the dust cloud). Dust clouds are treated exactly like smoke (see *Bolt Action*, pages 64–65 and 78).

EASY TARGETS

Bereft of cover, units in the desert make easy targets for aircraft. During a battle fought in the desert, when a player rolls on the Air Strike table (*Bolt Action* page 65), he can roll two D6 and choose the highest score as his result. However, if there is an enemy Air Observer on the table that has the Desert Fighter special rule, only one D6 is rolled for the Air Strike as normal. The observers have been trained to act as spotters, pinpointing enemy aircraft movement on the desert horizon long before they arrive.

In addition, such is the ease with which an aircraft can make its attack run against a target in the desert, that when an aircraft has attacked the original target, it can immediately attack another enemy unit within 6" of the original target (same type of aircraft, of course, simply apply the additional pinning based on that type of airplane and then roll again for number of hits caused, etc.). The only defence against this (and one espoused by General Patton in his *Notes on Tactics and Techniques of Desert Warfare*) is unit dispersal, where a commander ensures that his units are staggered at a sufficient distance from each other.

DUG IN: FOXHOLES, TRENCHES AND GUN PITS

In every theatre with suitable terrain all sides used gun pits, foxholes and trenches to defend their ground. In *Bolt Action* terms this means that defending units set up on the tabletop at the beginning of the game can have the advantages of Dug In positions. Dug In positions work a lot like the Hidden Set-Up rules in that regard, but in the case of Dug In positions the bonuses continue to function during combat.

DUG IN RULES

Where indicated in the scenario, units can be Dug In at the start of the game (for scenarios where it is not specifically mentioned as a rule of thumb a unit that can use Hidden Set-Up is allowed to be Dug In). These units must be deployed on the tabletop at the start of the scenario and may be subject to the Hidden Set-Up rules as well. Dug In units are still placed on the table in the usual way, and must be marked in some fashion to show that they are hidden – any distinct token or marker will do.

A Dug In unit counts as 'Down' when shot at, even if it's not Down (additional –1 to be hit and the number of hits from HE is halved rounding down). If the unit does go 'Down'

while Dug In, the benefits of being Down are doubled (i.e. –2 to be hit and only one-quarter damage from HE). Being Dug In offers no additional protection or benefit against enemy assaults (although tank assaults are an exception, see below)

Units count as Dug In until they're ordered to Advance or Run. If possible mark the locations of vacated foxholes, gun pits and trenches so that they can be re-occupied or captured by the enemy later. Card counters, plasticine or piles of small stones can be used as a makeshift solution, although gorgeous modelling solutions made with foamcore, clay or similar materials are preferred of course!

DUG IN VEHICLES

On the defensive it was common practice to dig in tanks as well as men, albeit considerably more digging was required! While the tank sacrifices its mobility, it gains protection by reducing its target size and not having its more vulnerable treads and hull exposed to enemy fire.

Dug In vehicles count as being in Hard Cover to attackers and count *immobilised* damage results as *crew stunned* instead. Dug In vehicles may not move during the game.

Italian troops dig in and take a breather.

DUG IN WITH HIDDEN SET-UP

A unit can be both Dug-In and use Hidden Set Up, providing it satisfies the deployment restrictions for both – in this case it is assumed the Dug-In unit has had the time and opportunity to properly camouflage its positions.

The Hidden Set-Up rules take precedence until they no longer apply, the Dug In unit does gain the additional protection of counting as Down against HE fire while Hidden. Once Hidden Set Up rules no longer apply to the unit for any reason, the Dug In rules apply instead.

DUG IN VS PREPARATORY BOMBARDMENT

In scenarios which use the Preparatory Bombardment rules (see Preparatory Bombardment on page 118 of the *Bolt Action* rulebook) being Dug In doesn't modify the effects of the bombardment. It's assumed that units are already taking cover as best they can from the bombardment and that in the event of a direct hit being dug in won't offer any additional protection from a heavy calibre shell, bomb or rocket.

DUG IN VS TANK ASSAULT

A foxhole or trench would give protection for a few moments, but if a tank actually stopped on it and twisted on its tracks a few times 'like a man crushing out a cigarette' (to quote one observer) the hole would collapse with messy results for the unfortunate occupant.

Models from Dug In units automatically pass their morale check and are not moved aside when assaulted by a tank as they simply duck down in their entrenchment and allow the tank to pass overhead. However, if a tank ends its Assault movement on top of any Dug In models those models are removed as casualties and the unit must take the morale check for tank assault as normal.

DIGGING IN DURING A GAME

We do not normally allow troops to Dig In during the course of a game, but if both players agree, troops can be allowed to go Dig In during a game if they are given a *Down* order. Make an order test for the unit at the end of the turn, if it succeeds and the unit remains on Down orders in the same spot until the end of the next turn, they will count as Dug In at their current positions in the end phase of that turn.

As this can slow down the game and makes some scenarios harder for one side to win we present it as an optional rule for experienced players rather than as a general rule of play.

CONTROL OF THE SKIES

Depending on the ebb and flow of military fortune, one side will sometimes have more or better planes available than the other. If this is the case, a player whose side has control of the skies can roll two dice when rolling on the Air Strike chart (*Bolt Action*, page 65) and can choose the best result.

Conversely, it follows that if one side has control of the skies, the other will be experiencing reduced air power – however, the enemy's aircraft cannot be everywhere at once, and a skilful or lucky pilot might be able to dodge hostile air patrols to reach the battlefield. If one player has control of the skies, the other player is still able to call an airstrike. However, instead of rolling on the Air Strike chart, he rolls a D6: On a 1–5, he gets a 'The skies are empty' result. On a 6, he gets a 'Here it comes!' result. Refer to the Air Strike chart on page 65 of *Bolt Action* for details on these results.

Note that this rule is different in essence from the United States' Air Power/Air Superiority rule. The US Army Air Force can enjoy air superiority without necessarily having control of the skies, but if it has both, this can make the USAAF a very potent weapon indeed.

GERONIMO! AIR-LANDING REINFORCEMENTS

The rules of *Bolt Action* deal with paratroopers and glider troops by assuming that they have dropped/landed outside the playing area and regrouped by the time they arrive on the table. We feel that the reserve rules, and particularly the outflank option, allow the player to simulate the situation where these troops arrive on the battlefield from an unexpected direction.

However, we have all watched movies where paratroopers land under fire and indeed there have been a few such instances in history, such as Operation *Mercury* in Crete. The optional rules presented here attempt to recreate those few dramatic occurrences in your games of *Bolt Action*.

PARATROOPERS – COMBAT JUMP

The units listed below can use the Combat Jump rules, even when they simply chosen as part of a normal Reinforced Platoon. They can do so even if they are chosen as part of an Armoured Platoon, in which case you cannot purchase a transport vehicle for them, much like cavalry and motorbike units.

- *Armies of Germany*: Fallschirmjäger squad (early war, late war)
- *Armies of the United States*: Paratrooper squad
- *Armies of Great Britain*: Paratroop section*
- *Armies of Italy*: Paracadutisti infantry section**
- *Armies of the Soviet Union*: Airborne squad
- *Armies of Imperial Japan*: IJA Teishin Shudan Paratrooper squad
- *Armies of France*: Groupe Franc/SES/GIA veteran infantry section**

* You can use this entry to also represent the Polish paratroopers of the 1st Independent Parachute Brigade that was created in Britain by the Polish government in exile and participated to Operation *Market Garden*.

** Use for 'what-if' scenarios, as these troops did not get a chance of being deployed through combat jumps in World War II.

AIRBORNE PLATOONS

To represent the various support units that were part of the airborne divisions, you can pick one or more platoons from the Airborne Platoon selector below. All units in this platoon have the ability to deploy using the Combat Jump rule. However, the entire platoon (or platoons) must deploy using a combat jump. Also all units must be chosen at Veteran level, or at Regular if a Veteran option is not available. Inexperienced units cannot be included in this platoon.

AIRBORNE REINFORCED PLATOON

1 Lieutenant (First or Second)
2 Airborne infantry squads (chosen from the list of Airborne units above)

Plus:

Headquarters
0–1 Captain or Major
0–1 Medic
0–1 Forward Observer (either Artillery or Air)

Infantry
0–3 Airborne infantry squads (chosen from the list of Airborne units above)
0–1 Machine gun
0–1 Sniper

0–1 Flamethrower
0–1 Anti-tank team
0–1 Mortar (light or medium)

Artillery
0–1 Light anti-tank gun, light anti-aircraft gun or light howitzer

COMBAT JUMP RULES

Units that choose to, or have to deploy through Combat Jump are left in Reserve (even in scenarios that do not allow this). When they become available, instead of entering the table from the player's table edge, they use the combat jump procedure below.

- The landing and roll distance: the player controlling the unit performing the combat drop places the Order die for the unit on the table with the directional arrow pointing to indicate where the unit is attempting to land and the direction in which it is travelling. The opponent gets to change the direction of the arrow by up to 45° clockwise or anti-clockwise. The player then rolls two dice. The sum of these in inches is the distance the marker is moved.
- When the final position of the marker has been established, place the first model of the unit in base contact with the Order Dice, touching the side of the dice opposite the one the arrow is pointing at (in other words 'behind the dice'). Then place all other models in the unit in a 'stick' of models 1" apart and in a straight line behind the initial model. Any models landing in impassable terrain are removed as casualties.
- Once all the models have been placed, the unit immediately suffers one pin marker. The unit's Order die is turned to the Rally face and the unit's turn is over (without actually executing a Rally order – this simply represents the airborne troops spending time regrouping). Enemy units in Ambush can now fire against the unit as normal, if they wish to. In addition, all enemy units that are not in Ambush and have flak weapons with a Pen value of +2 or less can fire these weapons for free against the unit (just as if they were in Ambush) – this does not require an Order, but can be done only once per turn.
- From the next turn the unit can fight as normal.

ALTERNATIVE RULES FOR PARATROOPERS

Instead of placing the Order die for the arriving unit and then rolling for distance travelled, you may hold the die roughly two foot above the table and let go.

If the die bounces off the table, the unit is placed back in Reserve and you will have to roll again for it next turn. Of course you can agree with your friends before beginning the game that any such incident means that the unit's transport plane has been destroyed instead, along with the unit – harsh!

If the die lands onto the table, proceed with deploying the stick of paratroopers as described above.

GLIDERS

Parachute landings were always problematic because they scattered the attackers over a wide area so disposable gliders were the airborne method of choice for delivering a coherent team for a raid on a specific target.

Gliders were nearly silent and very accurate, normally landing within one hundred metres of the target. They also delivered a concentrated squad with their equipment in the same package. The primary problem with a glider landing was finding a large flat area of land clear of obstructions near to the target to act as a landing zone.

Gliders were designed to drop steeply into the landing zone but the length of landing roll was always problematical. The main problem with gliders was that a hard landing could cause injuries to the troops on board, even rendering them unconscious or killing them. The breaking parachutes were a largely untested innovation that tended to tip the gliders nose down.

GLIDER LANDING UNITS

The units listed below can use the Glider Landing rules, even when they simply chosen as part of a normal Reinforced Platoon. They can do so even if they are chosen as part of an Armoured Platoon, in which case you cannot purchase a transport vehicle for them, much like cavalry and motorbike units.

- *Armies of Germany: Heer* Pioneer squad, *Sturmpioniere* squad, *Fallschirmjäger* squad (late war), *Waffen-SS* squad (late war)
- *Armies of the United States:* Paratrooper Squad, Glider squad
- *Armies of Great Britain:* Paratroop Section, Regular or Veteran infantry section (mid-/late war)
- *Armies of the Soviet Union:* Veteran squad, Airborne squad*

*Use for what-if scenarios, as these troops were not deployed by glider landing in World War II.

GLIDER LANDING PLATOONS

To represent the various larger glider-landing unit that were part of the airborne divisions, you can pick one or more platoons from the Glider Landing Reinforced Platoon selector below. All units in this platoon have the ability to deploy use the Glider Landing rule. However, the entire platoon (or platoons), must deploy through Glider Landing. Also all units must be chosen at Veteran level, or at Regular if a Veteran option is not available. Inexperienced units cannot be included in this platoon.

GLIDER LANDING REINFORCED PLATOON

1 Lieutenant (First or Second)

2 Glider Landing infantry squads (chosen from the list of Glider Landing units above)

Plus:

Headquarters

0–1 Captain or Major

0–1 Medic

0–1 Forward Observer (either Artillery or Air)

Infantry

0–3 Airborne infantry squads (chosen from the list of Glider Landing units above)

0–1 Machine gun

0–1 Sniper

0–1 Flamethrower

0–1 Anti-tank team

0–1 Mortar

Artillery

0–1 Light or medium anti-tank gun, light or medium anti-aircraft gun, or light or medium howitzer

Tanks, Tank Destroyers, Self-propelled Artillery and Anti-aircraft Vehicles

0–1 Tetrarch light tank (Allied armies only)

Transports and Tows

0–1 Jeep (any type, Allied armies only)

US Airborne jeeps

GLIDER LANDING RULES

Units that choose to, or have to deploy through Glider Landing are left in Reserve (even in scenarios that do not allow this). When a unit transported in a glider becomes available, instead of entering the table from the player's table edge, use the Glider Landing procedure below.

- The landing and roll distance: the player controlling the glider places a marker on the table with a directional arrow to indicate where the glider touches down and the direction in which it is travelling. The opponent gets to change the direction of the arrow by up to 45° clockwise or anti-clockwise. The player then rolls two dice. The sum of these in inches is the distance the glider moves before stopping. Move the marker or glider model accordingly.
- Breaking parachute: after observing the glider's roll distance, the player can choose to deploy a breaking chute. Roll a die. The number in inches is the reduction in roll distance. However the use of a braking parachute adds +1 to the landing impact die roll.
- Placing the glider: when the final position of the marker has been established, place the glider model (if you have one) with the nose on the marker and the tail pointing back towards the direction of entry. The glider counts as a soft-skinned transport vehicle that cannot move. If you don't have a glider model, use a 12"-long, 3"-wide rectangular marker, or alternatively you can simply place the models lying down in an equivalent area on the table and/or mark them with a token that identifies them as 'inside the glider'.

- Activating units in the glider: After the glider has landed, all units inside it have their order dice taken out of the bag, assigned to them and turned to *down* for the turn. All units are assumed to be in the glider, extricating themselves from the fuselage, counting as units embarked onto a soft-skinned transport. From the following turn, when you intend to give an order to a unit in the glider, first roll a die for that unit to see if it exits safely. Add any modifiers and apply the result from the landing impact table. At the start of each following turn roll again for any units still in the glider (same modifiers apply).

ALTERNATIVE RULES FOR GLIDERS

Make a paper airplane to represent the glider (using an A4 sheet of paper!), then instead of following the procedure described above, place your back to the table, walk a couple of steps away from the table and then turn around and throw the paper airplane onto the table.

If the paper airplane lands off the table, it is placed back in Reserve and you will have to roll again for it next turn. Of course you can agree with your friends before beginning the game that any such incident means that the glider has been destroyed instead, along with all the units it was carrying… very, very harsh!

If the paper airplane lands on the table, replace it with the glider model and continue as described above.

LANDING IMPACT TABLE	
DIE ROLL	RESULT
1–4	Section exits safely
5–6	Section is stunned and does not exit glider this turn
7+	Section is stunned and does not exit glider this turn; one man is badly injured, remove from the game (controlling player's choice)
MODIFIERS	
Deploying breaking parachute: +1 Striking a solid object such as a building, telegraph pole or gun pit: +1	

NIGHT FIGHTING

The following rules deal with the limited visibility and uncertainty caused by night operations. They can also be used for battles that occur in other situations of limited visibility, like heavy fog, snow blizzards, sandstorms and the like. We have found that these rules add a layer of complexity to games of *Bolt Action*, and slightly slow down game-play, but they create a very different gaming experience, with different tactical challenges and extra tension that, we feel, perfectly captures the fear and confusion of fighting at night.

DIFFERENT TYPES OF NIGHT FIGHTING GAMES

Whenever you are about to pick a scenario for a game of *Bolt Action*, you can agree with your opponent that the game you are going to play is going to simply follow the normal game rules, or that it is going to be a Night Fight, in which case the Limited Visibility rules (below) will apply throughout the game. Alternatively, you can decide that you are playing a Dawn Assault game, a Longest Day game, or a Flare! game.

If you cannot decide on which type of game to play, you may instead roll on the chart below at the same time as you roll for the scenario being played:

- 1: Night Fight
- 2: Flare!
- 3: Dawn Assault
- 4: Longest Day
- 5: Normal visibility game (or roll again, if both players agree)
- 6: Players roll-off and the winner chooses

DAWN ASSAULT

In a Dawn Assault, the game begins with the Limited Visibility rules, but you must roll a die at the beginning of each turn after the first, and add the current turn number to the result (e.g. add +2 on turn two, +3 on turn three, etc.). On a modified total of 8 or more, the Limited Visibility rules immediately cease to apply and visibility returns to normal for the rest of the game.

German troops negotiate an Italian mountain pass

LONGEST DAY

In a Longest Day game, you begin with normal visibility, but you must roll a die at the beginning of each turn after the first and add the current turn number to the result (as above). On a modified total of 8 or more, the Limited Visibility rules immediately begin to apply and last for the rest of the game.

FLARE!

In a Flare! game, the action takes place at night, with Limited Visibility throughout, but you must roll a die at the beginning of each turn after the first. On a roll of 4 or more, a powerful flare goes up (or series of flares are parachuted in, or a heavy fog curtain lifts temporarily…) and visibility is normal for that turn only. Roll again for visibility the next turn, and so on.

NIGHT FIGHTING RULES

LIMITED VISIBILITY

When you are determining whether a unit is able to see a target (for shooting, assaulting, etc.) at night, first follow the normal rules for line of sight. If the target would be visible according to the normal rules, then start the normal shooting procedure and declare the target. Then, before the 'target reacts' step, you must take a spotting roll for the acting unit to see whether they can actually identify the target through the darkness:

Roll 2D6 and add or subtract any of the modifiers listed below that apply, down to a minimum modified total of 2.

VISIBILITY MODIFIERS

- +6" The target has a 'Fire', 'Advance', 'Run' or 'Rally' order die on it.
- +6" The target has a 'Muzzle Flashes!' marker on it (see below)
- -6" The target has a 'Down' order die on it.
- -6" The target is a small unit
- +6" The target is a vehicle

If the modified total is equal or higher than the distance between the firing unit and the target, then the target is visible and the firing/assaulting sequence continues as normal – target reacts etc.

If the total is lower than the distance to the target, the attacking unit cannot shoot/assault the target and its action ends immediately (the acting unit's Order Die is simply left as it is), as the men nervously scan the darkness in search of targets.

MUZZLE FLASHES

The worst thing a unit can do at night is to open fire, as the loud noises and particularly the flashes of their weapons will reveal their position to the enemy. And tracer rounds are infamous for 'working both ways'. To represent this, when a unit fires any weaponry against an enemy, it must be marked with a 'Muzzle Flashes' marker (a coin or other token). This token makes the unit more visible, as shown in the chart above, and will remain with the unit until it receives another order.

Note that it is possible for a unit to receive a Fire! order die, but then to be unable to actually open fire (because of a failed spotting roll, for example). These units do not receive a Muzzle Flashes! marker – you only get one when you actually fire a weapon at the enemy.

FIRES

Burning vehicles or buildings illuminate a surprisingly wide area at night and anyone near them is very likely to get spotted. Count any unit within 6" of a building or vehicle that's on fire as having a 'muzzle flashes' marker even if they haven't fired.

REACTING TO AN ASSAULT

If a unit successfully declares an assault at night and the targets reacts by firing at the assaulting models, the target unit must first make a spotting roll to see if they can see the assaulting models (before they are moved). If the target unit fails this spotting roll, it may not react, just as if the assaulting unit was within 6" when they declared the assault – a blood-curdling surprise charge out of the darkness!

INDIRECT FIRE

If a weapon with Indirect Fire has 'zeroed in' on to a target, there is no need of making another spotting roll to fire at that target; simply roll to hit on a 2+, as normal.

FORWARD AIR AND ARTILLERY OBSERVERS

When an artillery observer calls in a barrage, it does not get a Muzzle Flashes! marker, as he's not firing any gun (unless of course someone else in his team does fire a weapon as part of the same order). When calling in a barrage, the observer does not need to make a spotting roll, but can instead place the marker anywhere on the table, as he would be relying on maps and noise/gun flashes rather than direct observation of targets. However, to simulate the increased chances of something going wrong, you suffer a -1 on the Artillery or Smoke Barrage charts (down to a minimum of 1).

Air Strikes cannot be called at all at night, making Forward Air Observers quite useless.

MINEFIELDS

MINEFIELD RULES

Players can decide to add minefields to any of their games, as long as they agree beforehand. Usually the defender in a scenario can deploy mines, since attackers are pushing into a new area and have not had the opportunity.

Initially, we are going to provide rules for visible, marked minefields, as we assume that both sides are adhering to the Geneva Convention and marking their minefields. We shall also deal by default with anti-personnel mines, as they are the most common. Later on we'll also provide rules for anti-tank, mixed, dummy and concealed minefields.

MINEFIELD SECTIONS

The default minefield section in *Bolt Action* is a 6"-sided square area. Larger minefields can be made by placing several of these sections next to each other.

Normally, we tend to allow the defender in a scenario two minefield sections per full 1000 points of his force. Or if you prefer you can allow a certain amount of points to be spent on minefields (up to 10 per cent of the force total), and say that each section costs 50pts.

A minefield section can either be a cardboard base appropriately decorated, much like an area of rough ground, or can be delimited ad hoc before a game using four 6" long obstacles (like a 6" length of barbed wire), or even simply using four counters set up at 6" distance to mark the corners of the minefield.

EFFECT OF MINEFIELDS

When any unit (friend or foe) moves into a minefield section, the opponent can interrupt their movement once at any point during their move, just as if the minefield itself was in Ambush. When the opponent declares that the minefield is 'attacking' the unit, the controlling player must halt at that point and note how much movement the unit has left. Assuming the unit survives its encounter with the minefield, it will finish its move as normal.

After the unit has been positioned at its 'Ambush' point, the opponent rolls one die to see if the unit triggers a mine, effectively rolling to hit the unit with the minefield section itself. A minefield section needs a 3+ to hit an Inexperienced unit, 4+ for a Regular unit, and 5+ for a Veteran unit.

Units belonging to the player that has placed the minefield are supposed to know the location of the mines, so they can force the opponent to re-roll any successful hit, as long as they are moving at an Advance. Also, units of combat engineers (Engineers, Pioneers, etc.) are trained to deal with these obstacles and always benefit from this re-roll when moving at an Advance, even when crossing the enemy's minefields.

If any unit (including friends and engineers) is sufficiently foolhardy to cross a minefield at a Run, the minefield rolls three dice when ambushing the unit rather than one!

If the minefield misses with all of its dice, the unit has not triggered a mine and can finish its move normally. If the minefield scores hits, then each successful hit is resolved with a Penetration value of +2 against non-armoured targets and +3 against armoured targets (Damage roll of 7+). Roll to damage as normal. A unit that is hit also suffers D3 pin markers rather than just 1. Note that the higher value Pen against armoured targets reflects the fact that the anti-personnel mine hits the weakly armoured belly of the vehicle – not normally considered

Italian armour passes a deadly obstacle

from the point of view of other hits.

If the unit is not destroyed, or broken by a resulting Morale check, it can finish its move as normal.

Note that a single minefield section can attack a unit only once per move, but can attack any number of units moving over it during the turn. Also, if a unit was foolish enough to cross two (or more!) minefield sections as part of the same move, each section can ambush it in turn.

ANTI-TANK MINEFIELDS

At the beginning of the game, you may secretly write down that any of your minefields is an anti-tank minefield. Anti-tank minefields only affect vehicles, and are ignored by infantry and artillery units that move over them. However, hits inflicted on vehicles are at +5 Pen rather than the normal +2.

MIXED MINEFIELDS

You can also create a mixed minefield section by 'using up' two of your sections. So, if for example you were allowed two sections in the scenario being played, you can lay both out as anti-tank or anti-personnel minefields, or deploy a single one as a mixed minefield. Make a note of which section is mixed.

A mixed minefield section combines the best of both worlds and will affect infantry and artillery with +2 Pen hits, but vehicles with +5 Pen hits.

DUMMY MINEFIELDS

You can replace any real minefield section allowed by the scenario with two dummy minefield sections. For example, if you are allowed two sections, you can place three down. Make a note of which sections are dummies. Your opponent might notice this variation in the number of allowed minefields, in which case he'll know some minefields are dummies, but of course he won't know which ones!

When units enter a dummy minefield, roll to ambush them as normal (including any re-rolls that the opponent may force upon you). If you score a hit, however, you have to reveal the minefield is just a dummy, and from now on it counts as a cleared minefield section (see below), as a few mines were often left even in dummy minefields.

MINEFIELDS IN WATER

As mines in shallow and deep water are intended solely to destroy boats and amphibious vehicles, you cannot place anti-personnel minefields in water terrain (Shallow or Deep), but you can place anti-tank minefields, or dummy ones, in either type of water terrain (see rules for movement in water on page 134).

CONCEALED MINEFIELDS

Instead of visibly deploying your minefields sections, you may halve the number of sections available and deploy them hidden without any markings. We cannot condone and do not encourage the use of this despicable practice, which is against the Geneva Convention!

Make an accurate note of where the minefield sections are. You can either use coordinates and/or make a map of the table as you wish. You cannot place hidden minefields in the enemy's set-up zone.

During the game, when a unit moves into the minefield, you must reveal it (the unit has spotted that something is amiss) and place it on the table, and then proceed to ambush the unit as normal.

BOOBY TRAPS

While a minefield is laid to protect an area, booby traps tend to be placed far more specifically at a choke point along a trail, for example, or at the entrance to a building with the objective of killing or maiming as many enemies as possible. As such booby traps follow the rules for a concealed anti-personnel minefield section with the following changes:

- The marker for a booby trapped area is a 3" diameter circle instead of a 6" square.
- When the booby traps are triggered they roll three times as many attacks as normal – so 3 against a unit on Advance orders and 9 against a unit on Run orders!
- Once the booby traps have been triggered and taken effect the marker is removed.

CLEARING MINEFIELDS

Once a minefield section has scored one or more hits on a unit passing over it, the opposing player rolls a die. On the roll of a 6, the minefield is **cleared**. If the unit that was hit was a vehicle with damage value 8 or more, the minefield is instead cleared on a 4+. This represents any subsequent troops either following in the tracks of the first or moving over craters left by previous exploded mines.

A cleared minefield is left in place, but from that point onwards the minefield only ever scores hits on a 6, regardless of the quality of the troops crossing it, and always rolls a single die 'to hit', even against units moving at a Run. Re-rolls for friends and Engineers still apply. This represents hurried mines clearance under fire, which is not exactly a thorough process, and might definitely leave a few isolated mines behind.

Thankfully, there are alternative means of clearing a minefield other than walking your infantry or driving your tanks over it. These are listed below with their rules.

MANUAL MINE CLEARANCE BY INFANTRY

Any infantry unit that has at least five models inside a minefield can be ordered to attempt to clear it using their bayonets. The unit must be given a special 'Mine clearing' order, which is the same as giving the unit a Down order – place a Down marker next to the unit and then make a 'mine clearing roll' applying all of the modifiers below. In order to clear the minefield section, the result needs to be a 6 after modifications. Note that a natural 6 is always a success and a natural 1 is always a failure. In addition, if a natural 1 is rolled, the minefield section ambushes the unit as normal (and in this case, an anti-tank minefield **does** affect the tampering infantry!).

MINE CLEARING MODIFIERS (CUMULATIVE)

- Veterans +1
- Inexperienced -1
- Engineers +1
- Mine-clearing gear* +2
- Per pin marker on unit -1

*Any Engineer unit may be equipped before the game with mine clearing gear (Bangalore Torpedoes, mine detectors, etc.) at a cost of +1pt per model, at least one of the models should show this upgrade.

BLOWING IT UP!

Any weapon capable of Indirect Fire can target a visible minefield section. Aim for the centre point of the section and roll to hit as normal (including ranging in for successive shots). If a hit is scored, roll for the HE value of the weapon – if you score at least 6 hits on the minefield with a single shot, the minefield section is cleared.

When resolving an artillery barrage 'Fire for effect' result, roll a die for each minefield section within range of the barrage (including concealed ones!). If you roll a 6, the minefield section is hit by a heavy howitzer as normal, and if you score at least 6 hits on it, it is cleared.

When firing a preparatory bombardment, roll a die for each minefield sections in the defender's set-up zone (including concealed ones!). If you roll a 6 that minefield section is cleared.

VEHICLES

LIMITED FUEL SUPPLY

The player's fuel supply situation is critically low. Whenever that player's vehicle wishes to move, roll a die. On a 1, the vehicle does not move and immediately counts as having suffered an immobilised damage result.

USING CAPTURED ENEMY VEHICLES

On all theatres of the war the combatants made use of enemy materiel that had been abandoned by the enemies as they retreated in a hurry or surrendered *en masse*. In North Africa, for example, the Germans used British and American

Refuel!

equipment and vehicles when they experienced extreme shortages of materiel, the Australians at Tobruk used captured Italian M11/39 and M13/40 tanks that they marked with large, kangaroo emblems on the hulls and turrets, and there's evidence of Polish tank crews using captured Panzer IIIs, respraying them with British sand paint and decorating them with British markings.

In terms of *Bolt Action*, a strict application of the rules for force selection does not normally allow you to field tanks and guns from other forces. However, we think it is great fun to collect a tank or a gun from an enemy force and paint it in your own colour scheme. So please feel free to undertake these fun modelling tasks, as I'm sure that your friends will not stop you fielding these vehicles in your force, as long as you pay the right points for them and they are taken simply to replace an equivalent 'slot'. For example, a British platoon could include a 'captured' Panzer with British crewmen, as long as it would take the 0–1 tank slot allowed for that platoon and the right points were paid.

As a rule of thumb, we tend to apply one further limit when we allow forces to purchase enemy 'captured' vehicles and guns. We say that the unit can be purchased only as

Inexperienced, or at best as Regular (if there are good records of a particular vehicle/gun being used in abundance by the enemy). This simulates the fact that the soldiers would be unfamiliar with the captured materiel, or if you prefer it can reflect the relative scarcity of its ammunition, spare parts, etc., which would make its use and maintenance trickier. If you really want, and you find an excellent historical reason for it, you can even allow the use of captured vehicles with a Veteran crew, but we feel they should then be penalised by adding the Unreliable rule to them (see below). This rule represents the same problems highlighted before, and ensures that only their rightful owners can make use of the vehicle or gun 'at its best', which seems just fair!

UNRELIABLE

A captured vehicle's or gun's chronic lack of ammunition and spare parts means it often suffers from extreme operational unreliability – if the unit suffers one or more pin markers as a result of an enemy attack, it automatically suffers one further pin marker in addition.

AMPHIBIOUS ASSAULTS

An over-the-beach assault against a waiting enemy is just about the worst way to enter combat. The rise and fall of the surf is constantly working against the attackers, while the defenders have a conveniently packed group of men against which to concentrate their fire.

When preparing to play a game of *Bolt Action* that involves an amphibious landing, you should define an area of the table as Deep Water, and another as Shallow Water. These areas of water normally start from the attacker's table edge, as described in the scenario being played.

MOVEMENT IN WATER

DEEP WATER

Deep Water is impassable terrain to all units except those that have the Waterborne or Amphibious rules, or any other rule allowing movement in water (i.e. boats and amphibious vehicles, usually). We assume that infantry laden with all of the kit they need to carry in combat cannot swim and keep their kit operational.

In addition the following extra rules apply:

- If a vehicle with the Waterborne or Amphibious rule is immobilized while in Deep Water, it will automatically drift D6" forward every time it receives an order.

- Units in Deep Water suffer an additional -1 to hit when firing their onboard weapons because of the waves rocking the boat. Players may agree to ignore this rule if the Deep Water in question is exceptionally still (placid lake, very slow moving river).
- If a transported unit does not have the Waterborne or Amphibious rule and is forced to dismount in Deep Water, it can try to reach an area of Shallow Water with his move to dismount. If it cannot reach the Shallow Water, it is destroyed.

SHALLOW WATER
Shallow water is treated as rough ground, with a few extra rules:

- Only Infantry and Waterborne or Amphibious vehicles may move in water.
- Artillery units treat it as impassable. If transported artillery is forced to dismount in Shallow Water, it can try to reach an area of solid ground with his move to dismount. If it cannot reach the solid ground, it is destroyed.
- While infantry are moving in water, they can do nothing else (e.g. an infantry unit may not fire weapons while in water).
- Infantry units must always pass an order test to execute an order while in water, even if they are not pinned.
- Water provides hard cover to infantry from small arms fire. This is due to the rounds being slowed down by the density of the water.

Even the feared MG42s bullets would stop after going through only 3 feet of surf!

- When an infantry unit finally moves out of the shallow water, it immediately gets an additional pin marker to represent the difficulty of regrouping after moving in water.
- Waterborne vehicles may end their move overlapping solid ground for up to half of their length, thus allowing transported units to disembark.

LANDING CRAFT

Below are the characteristics for the most common type/sizes of landing craft used in World War II – feel free to add them to any nation's transport force for amphibious operations. The standard rules for transports apply to landing craft, with the exception that units must begin the game on landing craft and cannot mount onto them unless the landing craft is partially on solid ground.

LANDING CRAFT, PERSONNEL

The most common example of Landing Craft, Personnel was perhaps the Higgins Boat. This ubiquitous vehicle was made from plywood, its design based around boats normally used in swamps in the mainland US. It could carry an entire infantry platoon or a light vehicle like a jeep and deliver them from their transport ship offshore to the beach, where the front ramp was dropped to let the troops quickly deploy. Around 20,000 were built during World War II.

Cost: 40pts (Inexperienced), 50pts (Regular), 60pts (Veteran)
Weapons: 1 MMG covering the front and left arc, 1 MMG covering the front and right arc
Damage Value: 6+
Transport: 36 men, or one jeep and 16 men
Special Rules:
- Waterborne: May only move in areas of Deep or Shallow water, being treated as a tracked vehicle for speed and turning ability
- Slow
- Open topped

Operation Lehrgang, the evacuation of Messina, by Howard Gerrard © Osprey Publishing Ltd. Taken from Campaign 251: Sicily 1943.

LANDING CRAFT, MECHANIZED

There were many different types of LCMs, but in general they were designed to deliver either a large body of troops or vehicles directly on to the beaches from their front ramp. They could carry a couple of trucks or even a single medium tank, making them a very useful tool during an amphibious assault.

Cost: 100pts (Inexperienced), 125pts (Regular), 150pts (Veteran)
Weapons: 1 MMG covering the front and left arc, 1 MMG covering the front and right arc

Damage Value: 7+
Transport: 100 men, or two soft-skin vehicles, or one armoured vehicle with damage value of 9+ or less
Options:
• Upgrade both MMGs to HMGs for +20pts
Special Rules:
• Waterborne: May only move in areas of Deep or Shallow water, being treated as a tracked vehicle for speed and turning ability
• Slow
• Open-topped

MUD AND FROSTBITE

MUD

Use these rules to represent any situation where the ground has been churned to mud by unrelenting rainfall, such as at Monte Cassino.

Areas of mud are normally treated as difficult ground in *Bolt Action*. However, if you like to add an element of randomness, you can agree with your opponent to use the rules below for vehicles and artillery units moving across areas of mud – vehicles and artillery units treat mud as open ground, but any such unit whose movement is going to cross a section of mud must declare their intended move and then roll on the Deep Mud table the moment they start moving onto the mud.

D6 ROLL	RESULT
DEEP MUD TABLE	
0	Buried deep: The unit cannot move for the rest of the game.
1–2	Bogged down: The unit has to stop, losing grip on the ground. The unit moves into the mud and then immediately stops (or does not move at all if it started the move in mud). The unit also suffers an extra -1 modifier to this roll the next time it moves.
3–4	Struggle: The efforts to cross this section of mud are very troublesome for your vehicle's traction. Vehicles continue with their move normally, but can only move through a maximum of 6" of mud as part of their move, after which they must stop. The same goes for Artillery units, except that they can move only up to 2".
5–6	Fairly solid going: This area was not as deep and soft as you thought. The unit continues with its move normally.
Deep Mud Modifiers Fully tracked vehicle: +1 Half-track: +0 Wheeled vehicle, artillery: -1	

FROSTBITE

In scenarios where the frostbite rule applies, affected units must take a Morale check at the beginning of the game. If the test is failed, each point by which it is failed indicates the loss of one soldier or crewman from the unit in the case of infantry or artillery, or immobilisation in the case of vehicles. If a vehicle is immobilised by frostbite while not on the table (including outflanking), it's considered destroyed – its passengers can arrive on the table on foot, but suffer an additional −1 to their test for coming on to the table (when such test is needed).